For Sheila and Wally,
With friendship and love.
Gilbert S. Rosenthal

GENERATIONS IN CRISIS

Gilbert S. Rosenthal

GENERATIONS IN CRISIS

Judaism's Answers

to the Dilemmas of Our Time

Bloch Publishing Company
New York

For Ann

"My beloved, my bride."

Foreword

That we live in an era when generations are in crisis cannot be gainsaid. Old values are crumbling before our eyes; cherished institutions are being assailed; long-accepted norms are being challenged and discarded. The crisis of our generations—both old and new—is severe, and the gap between old and new widens. Many of our leaders and thinkers, scholars and spiritual mentors are worried—and rightly so. Where will it all end? It there no way out of the morass?

I have made a modest attempt in this volume to deal with some of the challenges and dilemmas of our times that so severely agitate mankind as they are seen through the lens of Jewish tradition. Several of the chapters have appeared in various journals, although in different form; others originated as lectures. Each study is aimed at the layman: Consequently, I have avoided technical jargon and abstruse textual analyses. I have not attempted to be impartial or to present the facts in a clinical, objective fashion, although I have tried to be fair in my analyses and honest in my evaluations. But I am a rabbi, and as such I do not approach my subject *ex nihilo*. Therefore my own passions and convictions, biases and predilections will naturally shape my use of texts and fashion my conclusions. While I have endeavored to set forth what Professor Max Kadushin calls the "emphatic trends" of Jewish theology, law, lore, and insights, I could not avoid stamping these trends with my own subjective opinions and conclusions.

Other students and scholars may read the same texts as I and come to very different conclusions. So it always has been in Judaism, otherwise how can one explain that the same Biblical law or Mishnaic text gave rise to two, three, or even more different opinions? Clearly each student of Torah and each teacher of the Bible brought to each text his own experience, emotions, biases, and passions. The interplay of personality in the development of religion cannot be overlooked. That is why differences of opinion marked classical Judaism; that is perhaps its greatest asset. For God's word is like a hammer on a rock giving rise to manifold views and a variety of insights. In the words of the great Maimonides: "The gates of interpretation and speculation are never closed." But despite the many differences of opinion, all of our sages were of one mind in believing that Judaism does hold forth some of the answers to the problems and dilemmas that plague man. I share that conclusion most fervently.

In the course of preparing this volume I enjoyed the assistance, advice, and stimulation of many people. My devoted secretary, Mrs. Dorothy Bernbaum, typed the entire manuscript. My publisher and friend, Mr. Charles E. Bloch, President of the Bloch Publishing Company, offered invaluable advice and helped oversee the book through its printing and publication. My students and congregants prodded and stimulated my thinking and writing and helped clear away the cobwebs. "Much have I learned from my teachers, more have I learned from my colleagues, but most of all have I learned from—my students," was the wise observation of an ancient Talmudic sage.

Above all, my dear wife has sustained my spirits and criticized my efforts as only a loving mate can do. Appropriately, it is to her that this volume is dedicated.

G. S. R.

Oceanside, New York
February, 1969
Shevat, 5729

Contents

Introduction

WHEN Major Gherman S. Titov, one of Russia's cosmonauts, returned from the limits of outer space, he observed that he had girdled the globe seventeen times and had reached the furthest heavens, but "saw no God or angels." This proved, said Major Titov, that the teachings of Marx and Lenin are correct. There is no God, and religion is merely the opiate of the masses.

Similar disparagement of religion has been tried before. When the explorers of the fifteenth and sixteenth centuries found the earth to be round rather than, as the Church of Rome had taught, flat; when astronomers discovered that man and his tiny planet are not the center of the universe, notwithstanding the teachings of the Christian religion, the faith of many crumbled, and the seemingly impregnable ramparts of religion were breached. The same phenomenon took place when Charles Darwin's theory of evolution began to gain acceptance—the literalists resisted tooth and nail, while the naïve and precipitous proclaimed the demise of the Bible and the eclipse of God. In this new age of space and the atom, the cosmonaut's comments are fearsome manifestations of the new challenge to religion in general and to Judaism in particular.

Why does atheism grow from time to time? Why is modern man subjected to an age of disbelief, of public piety polluted by private paganism?

Depressingly enough, a challenge to theology by the most enormous evil known to man has shattered the beliefs of innumerable people. "For how can a good God," they ask, "have permitted so many wars, so much slaughter of human life within the span of the last half century?"

The bewildering behavior of a supposedly beneficent deity, however, has not sown the seeds of doubt among the millions; other influences have caused a decline in faith.

The decline today has been engendered by the progress, the advances, in the precise sciences. Because it has been discovered that mankind lives in a mechanistic universe subject to fixed laws and readily programmed into computers, it follows that belief in miracles is passé: How can there be a supernatural being or deity? In short, many scientists and their disciples believe there is no God.

Another reason for the decline in faith is the failure by organized religion to convince the young people. Youth is searching, it is questioning, and religion does not answer. Science, youth maintains, meets—and continues to meet—the demands of the times. Religion, in the eyes of the young, does not seem to be capable of meeting this challenge.

Man and his offspring, however, have been confounded by similar problems in the past. The first crude machines threw many of our ancestors out of work, just as the cotton gin displaced thousands of workers in the American South. The fear of annihilation is not new to man, either. War has been a perennial, human disease from Neanderthal times to the nuclear age, but the bow and arrow and the subsequent weapons of effective murder devised by man's misguided genius have now brought humanity to the *ultimate* weapon: a bomb capable of ending life on this planet. Who dared open this devastating, destructive Pandora's Box? And what can prevent annihilation? The answer lies in the past.

From the dawn of time, organized religion has been summoned to forestall man's destruction while abetting his salvation. One of the basic functions of religion is to help man to rise above the problems and perplexities of daily life, to meet the challenges inherent in the adventure of living, and to find meaning in existence. The most fecund and fearless minds of all religions have ever sought the answers designed to inspire and to save humanity.

Religions that have met the challenges of the agnostics and the attacks of the atheists and others with honest and visionary responses are alive today; those faiths that have failed to produce the proper guideposts for rational living have, like Jonah's gourd, withered on the vine. Thus Zoroastrianism, once a world influence, is all but extinct today because it refused to develop with the changing times. Hinduism and Shintoism are rapidly losing their grip over the faithful, and Buddhism is gravitating toward the museum of ancient—and dead—religions.

A living religion must speak, and it must answer. To its adherents and believers, religion must speak in meaningful terms. It must answer the questions of its adherents with clarity, with empathy, and with concern. Should religion fail in this, it will fail in everything and become an ossified relic of the past.

So far, Judaism has eschewed the two extremes that have caused the death of atavistic religions. On the one hand, Judaism has avoided the Scylla of petrified intransigence, and on the other, the Charybdis of anarchical caprice.

Realizing that Judaism's ship could not weather the storm while encrusted with sacerdotal barnacles, the Prophets of Israel underscored the moral factor in religion. They extolled the values of inner piety, of justice, of love, and compassion.

When the Temple was burned, the land decimated, the people enslaved and led into exile, Jeremiah, Deutero-Isaiah, and Ezekiel met the challenge by showing Israel it could sing the Lord's song on a strange soil. How clearly and admirably did these prophets demonstrate to their people that God could be worshipped without a Temple and without blood-sacrifices! And how marvelously did they instill hope into these exiles—the undying hope of a return to Israel's lost glory!

Oh yes! It was the actions of the Prophets, this forward step in the history of worship, that caused Israel to survive conquest, exile, and in this century, genocide.

The Pharisees, too, walked in the paths of the Prophets, for they created the protean world of rabbinic Judaism. They taught that a living Judaism required dynamism, boldness, and organic growth as well as a sense of continuity with the past and an anchor in tradition. They viewed their task with reverence and considered themselves to be legitimate interpreters of the Divine will. They applied themselves to the task of reinterpretation with sincerity, courage, and common sense. Hence they discovered a rationale for defensive wars on the Sabbath so that the people might "live by the commandments and not perish because of them." Their manifold decrees and ordinances and legal enactments and moral pronouncements were aimed at one goal—the perpetuation of this People we call Israel.

Even in the dark Middle Ages there were luminaries who stood out with bright courage and met the crises of the day boldly and fearlessly, who suffered contumely and criticism unflinchingly.

The great tenth-century Franco-German sage, Rabbenu Gershom, was responsible for the revolutionary changes in domestic law that outlawed polygamy and required mutual consent for divorces. The Spanish-Egyptian sage and philosopher, Moses Maimonides (1135-1204), came to grips successfully with the Aristotelian-Moslem onslaught on Jewish Philosophy and guided his perplexed coreligionists out of the quagmire of doubt.

Even the modern Hassidic movement, with all of its excrescences and superstitions, gave millions of Jews a sense of pride in their religion and rediscovered the inner worship of God in a community where formalism and frigid externalism had smothered piety and love of the Divine.

The French Revolution wrought monumental changes in Jewish life and thought. The gates of the ghettos were flung open; the independent "state-within-a-state" Jewish community was shattered; Jews were exposed to the world outside—to its ideas and doubts and challenges; civic and social emancipation was offered to the former pariahs of Europe. The Jewish civilization was unable to cope with the challenges: thousands fled from the mother faith; thousands converted, and many simply leaped into the sea of apathy and assimilation.

Why was Judaism so unprepared for the challenges of modern life and thought? Was it failure of nerve? Had seventeen centuries of exile and wandering, of persecution and degradation, of discrimination and contempt sapped our faith of its vital fluid and our people of its *raison d'être*? Had Israel, like mold, grown accustomed to the dark cellar of ghetto existence only to shrivel and expire in the light of freedom? Or had our culture grown so sensitive to the assaults of Church and Mosque that it was forced to cloak itself in medievalism?

There were attempts to meet the new age and its problems.

Reform Judaism sought to revitalize Jewish life and theology by Westernizing its orientation and discarding much of its ritual. Neo-Orthodoxy dressed up the old practices in modern garb, retaining the bulk of Jewish law. Conservative Judaism endeavored to steer a middle course between the two extremes, preserving much of the traditions, yet reserving to itself the right of reinterpretation. But all three schools of thought agree today that it is impossible to turn back the clock: Jews cannot return to ghetto thinking and living.

The challenges of the new age in which we live have perplexed Judaism before in different forms and magnitude, for as Koheleth wisely observed, "There is nothing new under the sun."

Children were impudent in 1200 B.C.E.; imperialists threatened the world with total war in Isaiah's day, and the rights of workers were trampled upon before the eyes of

Jeremiah. Each time, however, this faith we call "Judaism" rose to the occasion and found an answer to the plaintive pleas of the anguished and aggrieved, and it found the answers because the sages taught, "It is time to act for the Lord even if it means abolishing Thy Torah." Now Judaism must again find the answers in the age when the Bomb hangs over our heads like the sword of Damocles.

Once Frederick the Great of Prussia asked his chaplain for proof of the existence of God. "The Jews," replied the minister, "the Jews are proof of God."

The fact that we are still here on earth is indeed a miracle, proof that there is a God. Mightier empires are gone, consigned to the scrap heaps of history; great religions have fallen into eclipse and oblivion; yet tiny Israel has survived nineteen centuries of exile and oppression, of homelessness and wandering, of pogroms and concentration camps. It has even lived to see the rebirth of its ancestral home! Surely we see here the hand of God, the mystery of Israel known to Him alone, but we dare not rely on miracles alone.

I believe that Judaism must meet the challenges of our times with courage, with humaneness, and with insight, or else it is headed for oblivion. It is good to trust in God's providence, but it is also vital to act. Judaism must provide answers and norms for those in search. I am convinced that it can—if only it is permitted to speak, and if only its adherents and the world will listen.

I

Marriage and the Family

"It is not good for man to be alone."

GENESIS 2:18

SOMETHING has gone wrong with American marriage and the American family. The facts are bitter and nettlesome; they give cause for deep concern.

Our divorce rate has reached an all-time high: 10.4 per 1,000 couples as compared with 1.7 in Canada, and 2.8 in England. Between one-quarter and one-third of American marriages end up in divorce courts. We have over 400,000 divorces annually—one-half the world total! Many marriages end in separations; many homes are unhappy, dissent ridden, held together only by the slenderest of threads.

Sexual promiscuity has swung sharply upward. There are three times the number of illegitimate births now than in 1940. The venereal disease rate has risen 230 per cent from 1956 to 1965 and almost half of the reported cases occurred among teen-agers and young adults. The American Medical Association has declared that the rise has reached "epidemic proportions" in some large cities.

Premarital sexual relations are no longer viewed with

9

such fear and disdain as in the past. The several Kinsey Reports indicate that both male and female are not as chaste as formerly. Studies on the college campuses show that attitudes and practices of even middle-class girls (formerly Victorian in their morals) are changing. One survey indicated that 50 per cent of the female students have engaged in premarital sexual relations; another found that 38 per cent would like to see the college authorities prescribe birth control pills.

Marital infidelity is also on the rise—even among women. One professor of psychiatry expressed the view that infidelity is part of our present-day social pattern "—a symptom of society's traditional as well as rapidly changing fashions, mores, and values." Margaret Mead comes to the same conclusion in her book *Male and Female;* she writes that marital infidelity in America is rooted in our culture, because our society is supposedly built on "freedom of choice."

The instability of American marriage is also reflected in the increase in mental illness in our country, among old and young alike. With unhappy, unstable parents, is it any wonder that we have so many unhappy and unstable children? As Dr. William C. Menninger puts it, "The family, the home, is truly the maker or breaker of mental health in most instances."

Clearly, then, American marriage is in trouble, and the American family is floundering. As David and Vera Mace write, "Marriage is changing in East and West." And this applies, I fear, to Jewish marriages as well.

But is it changing for the *better?* I think the answer is obviously "No!"

Many are the students and scholars who have sought to

discover the reasons inherent in the crisis of the American family. We hear them talk of "the backlash of World War II," "the Age of Anxiety," "the Bomb," "the birth control pill," etc. To be sure, these *are* all factors in the problem, but there are even more fundamental issues that lie at the heart of the matter, and the sociologists, psychologists, clergymen, and marriage counselors who have studied the problem at close range have arrived at several conclusions.

There is little question but that parents are not exerting significant control over their children's dating habits and marriage patterns. The decline of parental control (especially noticeable in suburbia) has been accompanied by the increase in marital failures. In the past, marriages were generally arranged by parents, or often through matchmakers (they still are so arranged in many parts of the world), and the past record of marital happiness is far superior to our present one. Since parents can aid in the selection of a mate with greater maturity and worldly wisdom than can an inexperienced young person, it is apparent that happy unions are dependent upon the involvement of wiser heads. David and Vera Mace describe the matchmaking process in their volume *Marriage: East and West*. They point out that matchmaking was not so terrible as we moderns think; that greater parental control in the choice of mates made for far more stable and enduring unions than we in our free and liberal society realize. And they wonder whether our new emancipation and liberalization are a blessing after all.

Americans have devised a new method of mate selection called the "dating process." The theory is simple: At the age of fourteen or fifteen (in many homes, even earlier) boys and girls "date"—they go together to such affairs as dances, movies, and parties. In this way, a teen-ager can meet several hundred young people by the time he is eighteen. Out of this mass of humanity he will choose a steady date and eventually a fiancée. Finally, in the fullness of time, the couple will march to the altar.

Many students of marriage are sharply condemnatory of dating. The Maces call the process a "vast Noah's Ark." "The trouble with American marriage," write James Bossard and Eleanor Bole in their book *Why Marriages Go Wrong*, "is American courtship." It is artificial; it is too juvenile; it is too premature; it lays too much stress on such lesser values as romance, sex appeal, charm, and affluence. Parents are actually pushing infants into situations that are really for young adults. Seeking to compensate for their own social failings, these parents urge eleven- and twelve-year-olds to date, to wear lipstick and high heels, and to act like grownups. They offer their sixteen-year-olds their cars and expense accounts. They are amused and pleased when their teenager announces he is "going steady," not realizing that going steady should be the *final* step prior to engagement and marriage.

This game of dating and playing "grownup" is fraught with dangers: It leads to promiscuity and illegitimacy. If youngsters kiss at twelve and pet at fifteen, what can one expect of them at seventeen and eighteen? Going steady also cuts down shopping around and leads to early marriage. The average age of today's marriages is eighteen or nineteen for females, and twenty or twenty-one for males. All observers agree that juvenile marriages are less likely to succeed. Statistics indicate that half of our annual divorces occur among couples *under* twenty years of age, and the divorce rate of youthful couples is six times higher than that of those who marry at more mature ages.

Children are hardly equipped to engage in the serious business that is marriage. Marriage is not a game of "house" that little ones indulge in with the girl playing "mama" and the boy playing "papa." Furthermore, juveniles are not capable of making an intelligent choice of a life's partner. The mate one selects at eighteen is often not the one selected at twenty-five, and the virtues and character traits one emphasizes as a teenager are not the same as those one searches for as an adult. The tragedy is that early marriages are likely to increase rather than decrease as a result of the early dating process, social pressures, and the military draft.

Nor should we forget that college unions are inevitable as long as parents are willing to foot the bills, and as a result of the lengthy graduate training required of every professional man these days. A generation ago a man could have received a medical degree at twenty-two and could have earned a living by the time he was twenty-five. Today a doctor is fortunate if he can make ends meet by the time he is thirty. The biological and emotional processes make it unnatural—and undesirable—for a man or woman to delay marriage until such a mature age, but the fact remains that student marriages fail to an alarming degree. Economic, social, and intellectual pressures are enormous, and many fail either in their studies or in their marriages—or both. Margaret Mead decries subsidized marriages because "a man needs economic responsibility to be a man." In short, youthful marriages have a poor prognosis for success.

Marriage experts also stress the psychological mood of Americans that makes for poor marriages. Bossard is irked by the excessive, rampant individualism of Americans. The average American seems to be interested only in "what's in it for me?" He takes, rather than gives; he is egoistic rather than altruistic. Since successful marriage is the fusing of two individuals into a creative partnership, excessive individualism is the mortal enemy of domestic success.

Far too many young people also marry for the *wrong* reasons. Frequently, marriage is an escape door for rebellious teenagers anxious to shed parental control and strike out on their own. Often marriage is the solution to premarital pregnancies, and we cannot overlook the excessive stress on romanticism and sex appeal that pervades contemporary culture in movies, books, television, radio, and magazines. It has misshaped and distorted young people's notions of the ideals and motivations of marriage. The chic figure rather than the genuine character wins the male heart these days; the gleaming convertible, not the sterling personality, captivates the modern female.

Intermarriage—interreligious and interracial—is also on the upsurge and is greatly responsible for additional domestic woes and marital crackups. Students of the problem agree that intermarried couples have a poorer prognosis for success than intramarried people. The estimates range from two to three times as many failures (according to Albert Gordon's study in his volume, *Intermarriage*) to six times the number of intermarried failures suggested by Kennedy, Kirkpatrick, and others. Moreover, the children of mixed marriages suffer—they suffer psychologically, sociologically, emotionally, and religiously. They are not sure of their roots; they are uncertain of their loyalties. Judson and Mary Landis describe in their volume, *Building a Successful Marriage*, how college students whom they had interviewed suffered because of their parents' mixed unions. The centrifugal forces are so great against parents and off-spring in such unions that it is a miracle so many survive! As Bossard puts it: "Marriage between two persons of the same kind . . . has more promise of lasting success than one in which there are important differences." And Albert Gordon writes that the "chances of happiness in marriage are greatest for those culturally, socially, educationally, temperamentally, ethnically, nationally, racially, religiously alike." Similarly, Bossard reminds us that "marriage is not only the union of two individuals but also of two kinship groups."

Why is intermarriage on the upsurge and likely to increase greatly in the future? There are many factors.

We live in a free and open society where racial, cultural, religious, ethnic, and social barriers crumble readily. Marrying across the lines is simple and acceptable. Mobility and propinquity have hastened the process. There is little parental control, less family antipathy to intermarriage than a generation ago. Religious authority has slipped; respect for theological norms has reached a nadir. The homogenous culture in which we live encourages fraternization, intermingling, and marriage between the unlike.

A liberal spirit has gripped the land, especially on the campuses. This new liberalism has spilled over from politics and economics into religion and morals. The *avant garde* liberal proves his liberalism and open-mindedness by inter-dating and intermarrying. The new universalism and Utopianism of the collegian and intellectual have doomed racial and religious differences. One world is upon us!

Whatever the factors making for intermarriage, however, the upsurge—even among traditionally endogamous

Jews—is undeniable, and this phenomenon is bad for successful unions.

There is yet another factor that makes for the failure of American marriage: There is little genuine effort at making marriage work. Few of the family rituals that once served as cohesive factors, binding parents—and children—together, remain today. "People can best be held together," writes Bossard, "by doing things together."

Many couples have low boiling points. They throw in the sponge at the first crisis, and are prepared to divorce over trivia. Years ago divorce was viewed with disdain, couples thought twice before splitting up. Today Las Vegas, Reno, Mexico, and Hollywood have made a mockery of marriage and minimized the tragedy of divorce.

Another factor responsible for the low boiling point of couples is their inability to overlook failings in their mates. "Keep your eyes wide open before marriage and half shut after marriage," counseled Ben Franklin. Far too many people are unable to overlook shortcomings. Forgetting that marriage is not a reform school, they go to the altar to alter their partners. Instead of communicating, of talking out problems and smoothing over difficulties and disappointments, most unhappy couples surrender to frustration and failure. They cannot cope with the normal and inevitable crises of marriage; they fail to work at improving their relationship, and so communications break down, and the union is dissolved.

In sum, then, marriage counselors, social scientists, divorce lawyers, psychiatrists, and clergymen are worried about American marriage and the American family. "Marriage is serious business"—it cannot be treated cavalierly.

The facts remain frighteningly real: American marriage is in trouble.

The traditionally solid Jewish family is also in peril. The once rock-like structure of the Jewish home is chipped and fragmented; the surface shows strains and fissures. We Jews have not remained immune to the ravages. The Jewish divorce rate (traditionally low for centuries) is on the rise. Rabbis and marriage counselors attest to the fact.

Infidelity has also invaded the sanctity of the Jewish home. The phenomenon is not new; ancient and medieval Jewish sources indicate that cuckolds and libertines were not born in our century. The rate, however, is alarmingly higher than before, although Kinsey's studies clearly demonstrate that the tradition-oriented and observant home is still unsullied.

Intermarriage in the Jewish community is similarly rising. The much quoted figure of 7 per cent of intermarriage among Jewish couples is, tragically, no longer accurate. The surveys of Washington, D.C. and Iowa by Dr. Erich Rosenthal demonstrated that the percentage of second generation native-born Jews in Washington who marry gentiles is 17.9 per cent; in Iowa, the percentage climbed to a startling 40 per cent. Even worse is the fact that fully 70 per cent of the offsprings of such unions are lost to Judaism!

While Washington and Iowa are not representative of American Jewry, the qualified students of the problem— such scholars as Albert Gordon, Nathan Goldberg, and Marshall Sklare—are all of the opinion that inter-faith and interracial marriages *will* continue to proliferate. Undoubtedly one of the major factors making for the upsurge in exogamous unions is the changing attitude of the second, third, and fourth generations of American Jews. Our ancestors viewed intermarriage with horror; it was considered a *shanda* (disgrace), and pious parents mourned over a prodigal child as if it had died.

But today? The New Haven study of Ruby Jo Kennedy demonstrated that 57 per cent of parents opposed intermarriage, 22 per cent would accept such unions provided the offsprings were raised as Jews, 18 per cent were indifferent, and only 4 per cent would "sit *shivah*" (mourn the aberrant child as though he had died) and sever all relationships with him. Two generations ago the figures probably would have been reversed. As to the attitude of young people themselves, the Columbia University survey by Caplovitz and Levy indicated that 33 per cent of Jewish students interdate, and 15 per cent think it likely that they will intermarry. Although Jews are still more endogamous than Catholics and Protestants, their attitudes toward interdating and intermarriage are changing; their opposition is softening.

All of this bodes ill for the Jewish future, for as Abraham Geiger, the great nineteenth-century Reform scholar declared, "Every intermarriage is a nail in the coffin of Judaism." And these facts diminish the chances for successful unions since intermarriages are less likely to succeed than intramarriages.

Marriage experts are in accord that religion is a positive factor for successful marriages. They agree that men and women who take their religious faith and rituals seriously are less likely to be promiscuous, to intermarry, to be unfaithful, and to divorce. The salvation of American marriage lies in the realm of religion, and the Jewish concept of marriage is, I believe, the most humane and most relevant.

"It is not good for man to be alone," said the Lord, "I shall make a helpmate for him." With these sublime words the Book of Genesis [1] begins the tale of man and woman— Adam and Eve. The names *ish* (man) and *ishah* (woman) are almost identical; the etymology stresses the proximity, the intimacy of man's relationship to his mate. Eve was made from Adam's rib; she was bone of his bone, flesh of his flesh. No relationship is as intense or intimate as that between husband and wife; no relationship is as critical to the sane and safe society. No wonder that Genesis devotes thirty-eight of its fifty chapters to domestic matters!

What are the Jewish concepts and norms concerning marriage? Are they still meaningful for our tempestuous times?

Judaism propagates the view that marriage is the formation of a new primary relationship and the severing of the Gordian knot of parental domination. "Hence a man leaves his father and mother and clings to his wife. . . ." [2]

It is the miraculous and thrilling fusing of two creatures, two beings, two personalities into one while yet remaining two: ". . . and clings to his wife, so that they become one flesh." Herein lies, in the words of Erich Fromm, the paradox, the dilemma of a happy union: two creatures, yet one; one, yet two. The ideal fusion is one in which altruism replaces egoism, selflessness overcomes selfishness.

In addition to this, Judaism stresses that marriage must aim at the propagation of the species. "Be fruitful and multiply and fill the earth." [3] Children were considered the greatest of blessings; sterility the most grievous of curses. Three of the four Matriarchs were barren, and their anguish is legendary. "What can you give me, O God, seeing that I am childless?" [4] cried Abraham over Sarah's sterility. Pathetic, too, is the silent prayer a heartbroken Hannah murmured in the Shilo sanctuary importuning the Deity for an offspring.[5] Talmudic law even went so far as to countenance divorce after ten years of childless union.

Judaism appreciated, nevertheless, that marriage was designed to give man and woman not only companionship but also love. Alone in the Garden of Eden, Adam was in a bleak hell; united with his Eve, he found Paradise. The Bible abounds in idyllic love stories: Isaac's love-at-first-sight encounter with Rebeccah; [6] Jacob working for years for the hand of Rachel—years that passed "as a few days because of his love for her;" [7] Ruth's romance with Boaz; David's ill-fated passion for Bathsheba; the Song of Songs and its frank discussion of erotic love. Love and marriage were natural to the Hebrew. Koheleth enjoined us to "spend your days with the woman you love." [8] Mar Samuel urged older widowers who have already fulfilled the commandment of propagation to marry for the sake of companionship, and Talmudic scholars and sages encouraged marriage and married love, without ever denigrating or denouncing what they viewed as a natural and normal practice.

For this reason, Talmudic law generally refers to marriage as *kiddushin* (sacred)—an act of "consecration" or "holy matrimony." It never viewed sex (within a marital setting) as carnal or lustful or sinful. Other religions merely condoned such behavior and permitted sexual love as a necessary evil for breeding purposes, and as a concession to the weakness of the flesh. "Better to burn than marry," [9] declared Paul, who proclaimed he would rather be a eunuch in the Kingdom of Heaven than a father and husband. Celibacy is still the ideal of Catholic Christianity and several Eastern faiths. In our own times, Pope Pius XII extolled virginity and celibacy as superior to marriage.

Judaism unequivocally rejects this position. Rare was the bachelor; rarer still the celibate. Ben Azzai, the younger contemporary of Rabbi Akivah, was one of the exceptions. Once he delivered an impassioned appeal to his colleagues to observe the commandment, "be fruitful and multiply."

"Practice what you preach, Ben Azzai," retorted Rabbi Eleazar ben Azariah.

"You are right," the abashed sage responded, "but I am hopelessly in love with Torah and have no place in my heart for a woman." [10]

In ancient days a lad of eighteen was usually married off; [11] bachelors were thought to be half-men, their lives devoid of blessing or good. [12] It is averred that marriages are made in Heaven by God Himself, and that forty days prior to conception future mates are paired off and assigned. [13]

Our approach to sexual matters has been frank, yet chaste. Remarkably, the sages believed in a special angel of conception and passion named Lailah (literally, "night" —no doubt akin to the nocturnal temptress Lilith) and free sex play was approved by them. [14] Two festivals—the fifteenth of Av and, strangely enough, Yom Kippur—were designated in ancient times as mating days when maidens would seek out proper mates.

Immorality, nevertheless, was viewed with alarm and even horror. The seventh commandment proscribes adultery, and the Bible designates capital punishment for the crime. Similarily, all manner of immoral behavior is taboo: the

Book of Leviticus devotes whole sections to enumerating sexual sins such as incest, consanguinity, homosexuality, and zoophilia.[15] The woman suspected of adultery was subjected to a soul-searing ordeal in which she was made to drink bitter waters mixed with an anathema-inscribed scroll.[16]

Rabbinic Judaism was no less outraged by immorality than Biblical Judaism. "All things God can overlook save lewdness," declared the sages of the Midrash,[17] for "unchastity causes God's spiritual immanence to depart." [18] One of the three cardinal sins we are to avoid even if it costs our lives is the sin of sexual immorality. Undoubtedly these norms conditioned the Jewish female—and male—to a life of chastity and fidelity. Kinsey's studies have indicated that in the observant Jewish home, sexual morality is the norm.

On the other hand, polygamy was permitted. The heroes of the Bible had several wives—certainly several concubines and slaves—but the trend was away from both polygamy and polygyny, and in Talmudic times one wife seems to have been the norm, not the exception. In the tenth century the sage of Mayence, Rabbenu Gershom, abolished polygamy. He did so partly as a concession to the Christian culture, but he was also motivated by humanitarian factors: he realized that polygamy degrades the wife and disrupts the family. Monogamy has been practiced among occidental Jews ever since, and Oriental Jews have recently followed suit.

Charles Darwin once observed that "man scans with scrupulous care the character and pedigree of his horses . . . when he matches them, but in marriage he rarely takes such care." Judaism agrees completely; it underscores the importance of selecting the proper mate and looking for the wholesome virtues that make for a good union.

Parental control was omnipotent; the children rarely selected their mates and often never saw one another until the moment of marriage. The marriage broker (*shadkhan*) arranged suitable matches in many communities. The Bible indicates the extent of parental control, but it also displays a concern for the feelings of the lovers. Laban, for example, confers with Rebeccah regarding her desire to marry Isaac.[19]

The virtues one ought to seek in a mate are inferred from some of the Biblical tales. Eliezer knows that the damsel Rebeccah is suited for his master's son, Isaac, when she displays her kindness and hospitality in giving him and his camels water and fodder. It is said of Rebeccah that she carried on the religious traditions of her late mother-in-law Sarah; she lighted Sabbath candles and brought God's spirit into the home through her piety—an acute insight into the role of the woman in shaping the religious mood of the household.[20]

The Chinese believed that one should "marry the girl across the street" so as to help cement a blissful union; the Hebrews maintained that one ought to marry within the clan. "And there went a man from the tribe of Levi and married a woman of the tribe of Levi."[21] Thus does the Bible describe the union of the parents of Moses. The rabbis of the Midrash analyze the text as follows: "Why the stress on 'the tribe of Levi?' This teaches us the importance of family background in choosing a mate." So one ought to check the family credentials in choosing a partner and one ought to "descend a bit" in finding a wife lest the spouse feel superior to the husband.[22] Likewise, a match ought to be made between a couple of similar age. And (most significantly) one should never marry merely for financial reasons.[23]

Torah knowledge was a common credential for mating. "A man should sell one's possessions to arrange for his daughter to marry a scholar." [24] In Eastern Europe, not too long ago, parents would often select a promising Yeshivah student for their daughter and would subsidize both his studies and the marriage, frequently for many years.

Intermarriage was viewed with alarm and disdain. As early as the Patriarchs, endogamy seems to have been the rule, not the exception. Abraham cautions his servant Eliezer to choose a wife for his son Isaac from among the Hebrews, not the Canaanites. Ishmael and Esau married Egyptian and Hittite wives and embittered the lives of their parents. Prince Zimri fornicated with a pagan woman and was lynched by Phineas. The Book of Deuteronomy warns the Hebrews not to intermarry with the pagan tribes [25] lest they seduce the Hebrews to idolatry and immorality. Ezra battled valiantly against intermarriages during the fifth century B.C.E. because he realized that the identity of Jews and Judaism would be swiftly submerged beneath a tide of cultural and religious assimilation if the trend were not reversed.

Marriages out of the faith did occur nevertheless. Ruth is a case in point. There has been a strong admixture of non-Hebrew ethnic stock in our genes. How can we explain this apparent contradiction? The answer is that conversion to Judaism was required of the non-Jewish partner. As a result, our biological composition became variegated while our religious standards were unadulterated. Even today, in the most assimilated Jewish homes, intermarriage is shunned. Why? Perhaps Oscar Handlin is correct in his interpretation: "A man holds dear what little is left. When much is lost, there is no risking the remainder."

Jewish tradition and experience grasped the techniques needed for keeping a marriage on the right track. It placed the husband in the dominant position; ". . . and he shall rule over you" said God to Eve in stressing the superior position of the male in marriage.[26] The contemporary "emasculation" of the American male would have found little sympathy in the Jewish world. The Jewish husband was not, to be sure, to bully or brow-beat his spouse; he was expected to seek his wife's counsel and honor her person. "Love your wife as much as yourself and honor her more than yourself," admonishes the Talmud.[27] Wife-beating was considered a heinous sin and was almost unknown in the Jewish home. While the Jewish female was inferior to the male legally and socially (as she was in *every* land until quite recently), she was treated far more respectfully than her non-Jewish counterpart. Is there a more beautiful encomium of the woman than that in the thirty-first chapter of Proverbs, where the "woman of valor" is described in such glowing terms?

When domestic difficulties erupted, compromise and arbitration were evoked. Frequently the rabbi was sought out as the marriage counselor, and the incident of divorce was amazingly low. The Jewish family, for all of its deficiencies, held together as firmly as the Rock of Gibraltar; it became an object of admiration in gentile eyes.

Love was not lacking in the Jewish home, but it came, curiously, *after* marriage. "And Isaac took Rebeccah to his tent as his wife and he loved her. . . ."[28] Samson Raphael

Hirsch, noting the unusual order in the text, stresses that love came *after* marriage in contrast to the contemporary emphasis on love and romance *before* marriage. It is the frothy love that evaporates and disappears with the passing of time; the truly solid unions deepen their stakes of love with the passing years.

Of course, Judaism was not so naïve as to assume 100 per cent success in matrimony. Divorce is expressly permitted in the Hebrew Bible: "A man takes a wife and possesses her. She fails to please him because he finds something obnoxious about her and he writes her a bill of divorcement, hands it to her, and sends her away from his house. . . ."[29]

The ambiguity of the passage gave rise to controversy over the grounds for divorce. The stringent view represented by the School of Shammai insisted that adultery or immoral behavior be the sole grounds for divorce. Hillel, on the other hand, asserted that even if a woman so much as burned the soup, her husband might divorce her. Rabbi Akivah seems to have gone farther: he permitted divorce if the husband found a more beautiful and desirable female.[30] All sages concurred that a man *had* to divorce his wife if she fornicated or flouted Jewish law and traditions.

The liberal views of Hillel and Akivah ought not to be taken too literally; what they were implying was that where love is dead and enmity reigns, divorce might be preferable to an unholy and embittered alliance. The liberal position prevailed; many were the grounds on which divorce was granted.

Safeguards were adopted, nevertheless, to prevent hasty or ill-conceived divorces. Early in our history, the woman received a marriage contract (*ketubah*) that assured her of an alimony or widow's settlement. The procedure of drawing up a bill of divorce (*get*) was excruciatingly complicated and time consuming. And Rabbenu Gershom of Mayence went farther: he insisted that no wife could be divorced without her consent.

On the other hand, a wife could not issue a *get* to her husband. This serious inequity still exists and places the Jewish woman at a distinct disadvantage. Still, she could sue for divorce on various grounds, among them incompatibility, impotence, noxious disease, odious occupation of the husband, failure to live up to marital and conjugal duties, and lack of support. In fact, the Jewish court in Talmudic and medieval times would force obstreperous husbands to issue bills of divorce to estranged wives.

Clearly, then, the prevailing Jewish view recognized that a marriage held together by sham, legal technicalities, the coercive power of the state or religion, was no true union. Contrast this position with that of Catholic Christianity (and some Protestant sects as well) that no man can "rend asunder what God hath put together." [31]

Unfortunately, divorce laws in several American states have failed to respond to human needs and have followed the Christian—rather than the Jewish—position. Consequently, divorce courts have become nothing but settings for perjury and collusion, hypocrisy and fraud. Staged "raids" or "lover's trysts" provide "evidence" of adultery for many; the more affluent fly to Reno or Miami or Mexico City for a quickie divorce. What a travesty on marriage! Would not society be better off with the humane and sane approach to divorce that Judaism offers?

Remarkably, although Judaism was liberal in granting divorces, the divorce rate in the Jewish community was—and is—notably low. Why? For one thing, because sacred matrimony was not a thing to discard cavalierly; for another, we appreciated the shame and tragedy of marital breakup. "When a man divorces his wife even the stone altar of the Temple weeps." [32]

The Jewish family and home stood out always as bright stars in the firmament, as examples to all peoples and religions. "The society of scholars and the family are like a stone roof," observed our sages.[33] "Remove a stone and it collapses; add burdens and weights and it endures solidly and firmly." *Shalom bayit* (domestic peace) was our ideal, for we concurred with Rabbi Simeon bar Yohai's view that "domestic strife is worse than the war of Gog and Magog." [34]

Is it not possible that the Jewish concept of marriage might hold forth the cure for what ails American marriage? Is it not plausible that a people that has always boasted of happy unions, low divorce rates, little marital discord, no wife beating, rare instances of infidelity—might have discovered the key to marital bliss?

Surely courses in marriage and the family in schools are valuable. And naturally, a code of sexual behavior for collegians might help the solution of our problem. But the fundamental causes of divorce and disharmony will not have been eradicated. The answers are the old Jewish answers: more parental control in selecting mates; greater stress on character traits in choosing a partner for life; marriage with similar kinds; better channels of communication in marriages; less haste in rushing off to divorce courts; greater stress on the sacred nature of matrimony. These are Jewish insights into how to achieve the successful union. The Prophet Hosea, shattered by a tragic marriage to a faithless wife, summed up the prescription for the happy marriage: "And I shall betroth thee unto me forever, and I shall betroth thee unto me with righteousness and justice, with love and compassion. And I shall betroth thee unto me with faith—and you shall know the Lord." [35]

The nuclear element of society is the home; the happy home makes the happy society. Even the Soviet Union has realized this; after bitter frustrations with its experiment in free love and simple divorces, the Communists have veered back to the traditional notions and norms. Judaism has always taught by precept and example that nothing is as beautiful as the happy marriage and the serene household. Marriage is too precious, too important to be handled with disdain. Love is the "flame of God." [36] Like a flame it can warm and brighten; but it can also sear and destroy. The future of the sane society depends on a sane approach to marriage that will illumine our lives and world.

NOTES

[1] Genesis 2:18
[2] Genesis 2:24—end
[3] Genesis 1:28
[4] Genesis 15:2
[5] I Samuel 1
[6] Genesis 24:67
[7] Genesis 29:20
[8] Koheleth 9:9
[9] I Corinthians 7
[10] Tosefta Yevamot VIII, 5; Genesis Rabbah XXXIV, 14
[11] Avot IV, 24
[12] Yevamot 62b-63b
[13] Sotah 2a
[14] Nidah 16b; Nedarim 20b; Maimonides, *Guide for The Perplexed*, II, 6
[15] Leviticus, 19, 20, etc; Deuteronomy 22:10-29 and 23:1-7
[16] Numbers 5:11 ff.

[17] Leviticus Rabbah XXIII, 8
[18] Sifré Deuteronomy § 258, p. 121a
[19] Genesis 24:27
[20] Genesis Rabbah LX, 16
[21] Exodus 2:1
[22] Yevamot 63a
[23] Kiddushin 70a
[24] Pesahim 49a
[25] Deuteronomy 7:1-4
[26] Genesis 3:16
[27] Yevamot 62b
[28] Genesis 24:67
[29] Deuteronomy 24:1 ff.
[30] Mishnah Gittin IX, 10
[31] Matthew 19:3-11
[32] Gittin 90b
[33] Genesis Rabbah C, 7
[34] Berakhot 7b
[35] Hosea 3:21 and 22
[36] Song of Songs 8:6

II

Birth Control

"Be fruitful and multiply and fill the earth."
GENESIS 1:28

IF THE demographers and sociologists are correct in their predictions, mankind will destroy himself with the population bomb rather than the Hydrogen bomb. The population explosion has been phenomenal: between 1900 and 1950 the world's inhabitants increased from one to two and a half billion. As of this writing, there are over three billion human beings on this planet. We add five thousand souls to that figure each hour and sixty million yearly. If the present trend continues, we can expect over six billion people on earth by the year 2,000.

This is a phenomenon that had already been noted over a century ago by Malthus, who wrote that population increases geometrically while food supplies increase merely arithmetically. Hence, wars, plagues, and other "leveling processes" serve the useful purpose of preventing men from overpopulating the earth and denuding it.

Prophets of gloom and doom in our day are even more dour than Malthus. They tell us that we are exhausting our

food and arable land; that famine and disease will ravage
not just over-populated nations like India, China, and Japan, but Western lands as well. They warn against unwanted children who are abandoned or aborted, or worse,
are raised to a life of crime, disease, malnutrition, illiteracy,
grinding poverty, and Communism. In 1955 in Japan, 67
per cent of pregnancies were terminated by abortion; in
our own country, it is estimated that one million pregnancies are illegally ended each year and most of these criminal
abortions are performed on *married* women!

To round out the gloomy side of the story of the population bomb, scientists at the Rockefeller Institute in New
York warn that overpopulation leads to aggression, hostility,
and other antisocial acts. A study of overcrowding in mice
communities showed that homosexuality, murder, and even
cannibalism resulted. The implication is that if the present
trend is unchecked, we will witness brutal wars of aggression launched by hungry people from Asia (notably Red
China) who will be forced to prey on their neighbors to
obtain food and *Lebensraum*.

We must not assume that these dark predictions and
pessimistic prophecies are the creations of irresponsible and
misguided amateurs and alarmists. Dr. John Rock, the famous Harvard gynecologist who helped develop the oral
contraceptive pill, and who is himself a devout Catholic,
testified before the Senate Government Operations Subcommittee that "present population growth rates on this
planet present an obviously lethal threat to all that civilization has achieved."

At the same hearing, Dr. George B. Kistiakowsky,
formerly President Eisenhower's special Assistant for Science, and William H. Draper, who was in charge of the

Draper Report on United States Foreign Aid in 1959, also took the view that prevention of a world population explosion is as great a problem as prevention of a nuclear holocaust. Anthropologist Margaret Mead warns against our present way of life, which "will ultimately turn the earth from a habitable place into a grim, overcrowded prison where individuals will survive only by stepping over the bodies of those struck down by hunger and despair." Even former President Eisenhower, who in 1959 rejected the Draper Report that urged our country to disseminate birth control devices among recipients of our aid, has changed his position and has publicly espoused the cause of birth control in overpopulated areas. And the eminent biologist Sir Julian Huxley warns that "death control has made birth control a moral imperative as well as a social and economic necessity."

Arrayed against these forces, we find some of the leading spokesmen for the religions of the world. For a long time the Protestant sects opposed birth control. In fact, the anti-birth control laws of New York, Connecticut, Massachusetts, and various other states in our nation, were the creatures of Protestant probity of the seventeenth, eighteenth, and nineteenth centuries. The Protestant churches have of late, however, changed their views and, with few exceptions, have supported the idea of family planning and utilization of contraceptive devices.

The Roman Catholic Church has remained steadfast in its opposition to contraception (although it has come to the point of recognizing the need for family planning) despite the fact that Catholics use contraceptives "in about the same measure" as their Protestant and Jewish neighbors, according to Catholic surveys. The position of the Roman

Church is that the primary purpose of marriage is procreation, and that no artificial means of frustrating conception may be used by the faithful. The Church considers contraceptives to be "intrinsically vicious" (the words are those of Pope Pius XI) and a violation of "natural law." The Church has come to realize, however, the need to limit the size of families, and it suggests the use of continence based on the cyclical or "rhythm method" whereby the couple abstains from coitus during the wife's ovulation period. Unfortunately, this method is only 40 to 50 per cent effective. Furthermore, the Catholic hierarchy has called upon the nations to find new food supplies and a better means of food distribution to the needy. The final word of the Church of Rome has not been uttered, however. Pope John XXIII organized a special commission to study the problem, and Pope Paul VI has continued in his footsteps. Some time ago, eighty-one Nobel Prize winners (including Roman Catholics) petitioned the Pope to review the teachings of the Church on the question, and the Pope's special fifty-six-member commission recommended a liberalization of the Church's position on the problem. Regrettably, Paul issued an encyclical in 1968 that reaffirmed the Church's traditional view that birth control is immoral and tends to make women into instruments of pleasure. By implying that birth control lowers the morality of the family unit, the Pope evoked a storm of protest from Catholics as well as non-Catholics, and unprecedented criticism has been levelled against Paul by Catholic priests and laymen. Consequently, it is not inconceivable that the Church may ultimately reverse its position that only the rhythm method is in consonance with natural law.

The birth control issue has become one of the heated

causes célèbres of our time in the legal, moral and theological realm. The recent Supreme Court decision that struck down Connecticut's law outlawing the sale of birth control devices or instruction in their use has laid to rest the legal question once and for all. The Court found that such laws are unconstitutional and unwarranted intrusions upon the privacy of citizens. Speaking for the majority, Mr. Justice Douglas wrote:

> *We deal with a right of privacy older than the Bill of Rights—older than our political parties, older than our school system. Marriage is a coming together for better or for worse, hopefully enduring, and intimate to the degree of being sacred. The association promotes a way of life, not causes; a harmony in living, not political faiths; a bilateral loyalty, not commercial or social projects. Yet it is an association for as noble a purpose as any involved in our prior decisions.*

But if the Supreme Court has settled the constitutional aspects of birth control, the moral aspects are still very much in dispute. Perhaps the Jewish position holds the key to the puzzle.

The Jewish view on propagation and birth control is based on two basic Biblical texts. One is the verse in Genesis 1:28—"Be fruitful and multiply and fill the earth." The sages deduce that this commandment laid upon Adam and Eve was the first *mitzvah* (commandment) of the Torah. Perhaps in order to replenish the waning Jewish population, sadly depleted by the Roman Wars, and perhaps, too, in an attempt to discredit the widespread use of contraceptives and abortions among the Romans, the Gnostics, and the Marcians, the sages of the Talmud never ceased to extol the importance of procreation. To further bolster their view, they cited the text in Isaiah 45:18 which reads: "For thus saith the Lord that created the heavens, He is God that formed the earth and made it, He created it not a waste—He formed it to be inhabited." In line with this thinking, the sages of Rabbinic Judaism sharply condemned, as we have seen, celibacy and bachelorhood.

The second Biblical passage relevant to our problem is the section in Genesis 38:8ff. We read that Onan was expected to marry the widow of his childless brother so as to "perpetuate his name in Israel." This practice of levirate marriage (*Yibbum,* as it is called in Hebrew) goes back to hoary antiquity, and is still observed in some Jewish communities. But Onan refused to carry out the Divine mandate, and instead, "spilled his seed on the earth." Death was the punishment meted out to Onan. On the basis of this text, Judaism severely condemned the practice of Onanism —some sages going so far as to indulge in the obvious hyperbole of equating it with adultery or even murder! The simple sense of the passage indicates, however, that Onan's sin lay not in wasting sperm *per se,* but rather in his refusal to discharge his religious obligation to marry his sister-in-law and produce an issue to carry on his late brother's name. Still, the Jewish tradition condemned the needless wasting of semen as a heinous offense.

It is instructive to note how later tradition developed these themes. The schools of Shammai and Hillel, for example, debated the matter of how many children one had to sire to fulfill the precept of fruitfulness. Shammai insisted on two sons; Hillel was content with a son and a daughter. The law is according to Hillel.[1] It would appear

from this that one is permitted to practice birth control
once the basic minimum family has been established. On
the other hand, Rabbi Joshua (second century C.E.) was
of the opinion that one should produce offspring even later
in life after having raised a family, on the basis of the text
in Koheleth 11:16: "Sow your seed in the morning, and do
not slacken your hand in the evening." Most authorities
agree, however, that only the male is obliged to be fruitful;
the female is under no such obligation, and hence is permitted to waste her ova.

The Talmud considers the health of the mother and the
welfare of the children in dealing with exceptions to the
general rule against destroying seed. In the classic passage
in Yevamot 12b and elsewhere we read: " 'Three categories
of woman may use a diaphram,' says Rabbi Meir. 'They
include a minor (lest she die in childbirth), a pregnant
woman (lest she abort or injure the fetus), and a nursing
mother (lest she neglect her infant and cause his death).'
The sages, however, do not permit the use of a diaphragm
and urge her to pray for Divine protection." Although the
law usually follows the majority against the minority or the
individual, in this case later tradition accepts Rabbi Meir's
position. Most scholars interpret the controversy to mean
that Rabbi Meir *requires* the use of a contraceptive whereas
the sages *permit* its use. The Talmud also records that
Rabbi Hiya's wife drank an oral contraceptive because she
suffered extreme pain in childbirth.[2]

On the basis of these texts and the discussions they engendered, medieval and modern sages came to the following conclusions: First, all concur that where there is danger
to the life of a mother, she may use a diaphragm or an oral
anovulent as prescribed by a physician; second, some even

permit the male the use of a contraceptive, although the sperm is thereby denied natural entry to the female; third, there are reputable scholars who allow *all* women to use contraceptives as they see fit since their use of anovulents does not constitute a breach of natural law; fourth, the great sixteenth-century Polish authority, Rabbi Solomon Luria, permits the use of contraceptives where there is a danger of producing immoral or degenerate progeny.

Furthermore, Jewish tradition did not consider procreation to be the sole *raison d'être* for marriage. As we have seen earlier, the Jewish view of marriage held that man and woman come together in union for the sake of love, companionship, and sexual fulfillment. For this reason, the majority of the scholars permitted a man to marry a minor, an old woman, or a barren wife where no possibility of procreation exists.[3] In sum, Judaism views procreation as one of—but not the only—motifs in marriage.

Today, only the ultra-Orthodox fringe in Jewish life opposes the use of contraceptives. The moderate Orthodox, Conservative, and Reform groups have all recognized that birth control has a necessary role to play in a happy and healthy society. If rabbinic scholars permitted contraception where a danger to the mother's health exists, or where the future and present progeny might be neglected or abused or their health impaired, by analogy we can conclude that we have a right and duty to prevent the birth of unwanted children, or children who will lack adequate food, housing, health facilities, and love. Each child born into this world has the natural right to the pursuit of life, liberty, health and happiness; when that opportunity is closed to him *ab initio*, when the results of his birth would be psychological trauma for his parents and physical deprivation for the infant, it would be better for him never to see the light of day. The sages of the fourth century appreciated this harsh—but moral—fact when they declared: "If famine and calamity come to the world, set your wife apart and abstain from relations" for "you cannot indulge in building a world when God is destroying it." [4] In our own day, Rabbi Naphtali Oshri permitted Jewish couples entombed in the Hell of Nazi ghettos normal sexual relations with contraceptives in the belief that it would be sinful to bring children into such a world but equally wrong to prevent husband and wife from enjoying sexual love.[5]

Some advocates of birth control suggest legalized abortion as a technique for population control—as well as a means of eliminating unwanted, illegitimate, and deformed infants. Indeed, there are countries in which abortion serves these purposes. Advocates of liberalized abortion laws point to the huge number of criminal abortions performed yearly (over a million in the United States)—not to mention the tragic number of deaths that result from such illicit operations (over 2,000 annually in New York State alone).

Judaism is unequivocally opposed to abortion as a means of controlling excess population.

On the other hand, Judaism is humane and liberal in matters of *therapeutic* abortions. The Mishnah teaches us: [6] "If a woman is in hard travail, one cuts up the child within her womb and extracts it member by member because her life has priority over its life. . . ." Clearly, the sages knew of the dilemma of mother's life versus child's; their decision was emphatically for the *mother's*.

Later authorities permit, or even require abortions, in matters involving the mother's mental or physical health—not to mention her very survival.

The tragic problem of a deformed or retarded fetus is also pertinent to the question of abortion. Mothers who have contracted German measles early in pregnancy face the strong possibility of blind, deformed, or retarded infants. Chief Rabbi I. J. Unterman of Israel has ruled against abortions in such cases. But the late Rabbi Yehiel Weinberg of Montreux, Switzerland took a liberal view. He ruled that the fetus is not yet a person and he permitted abortions. Abortions are also allowed when conception results from rape; they are not permitted, however, when the conception results from adultery "lest we open the floodgates to immorality and debauchery."

Consequently, therapeutic abortions are permitted, and in some instances, even required by Jewish law. But feticide is definitely not a proper or moral means of controlling population.

Although the Jewish tradition adopts a reasonable and humane attitude on the question of birth control, it does not neglect the other side of the coin—namely, the problem of infertility. As we have noted, Jewish tradition maintained that the worst affliction that can befall a couple is sterility and childlessness. Dr. Abner Weisman, Clinical Professor of obstetrics and gynecology at New York Medical College, estimates that one out of ten couples in our world is childless. And most, undoubtedly, would give anything to have a youngster on whom to lavish love and warmth, material and spiritual well-being. Weisman points out that we have expended millions of dollars to solve the problem of fertility and ease the suffering and anguish of couples capable of reproducing, but we have allotted scarcely a pittance to give fulfillment to those desirous of and financially and morally capable of raising children. In short, we are in need of a breakthrough in the area of infertility comparable to the breakthrough in the realm of contraception. This is particularly urgent for the Jewish people, whose birthrate is traditionally too low and whose ranks have been decimated by one-third in our own days. Wanted children as well as unwanted children pose bitter and thorny challenges to medical science and theology alike. But surely the same human genius that split the atom and invaded the cosmos is capable of finding solutions. If not, then Isaiah's dream world of happy habitation will become a nightmare world of void and emptiness, of waste and desolation.

NOTES

[1] M. Eduyot I, 13; Gittin 41b; Yevamot 61b
[2] Tosefta Yevamot VIII, 2; Yevamot 65b
[3] Ketubot 39a; Rabenu Tam, cited in Tosafot Yevamot 12b, etc.
[4] Yerushalmi Taanit I, 6; 65d; Genesis Rabbah XXXI, 12 and XXXIV, 7; Tanhuma *Noah* pp. 21b-22a
[5] *Sheelot u-Teshuvot Mi-Maamakim*, Number 18
[6] Ohelot VII, 6

III

Juvenile Delinquency

"Children I have reared and brought up,
and they rebelled against Me."

ISAIAH 1:2

The affluent society which we enjoy is not necessarily the happy society. There abound in it much unhappiness, much ennui, much dissatisfaction, and many tensions.

Just look at our young people! Our children and adolescents are in turmoil; we are witnessing a "delinquent generation," a shook-up generation, a world of kids in conflict with their parents, their teachers, their societies, their religions, and their norms.

Is it a new phenomenon? Evidently not. An Egyptian priest, writing in 2,000 B.C.E., records: "Youth is disintegrating. The youngsters of the land have a disrespect for their elders, and a contempt for authority in every form. Vandalism is rife, and crime of all kinds is rampant among our young people." The Bible wrestled with the matter of the "rebellious and contentious son," and Socrates bemoaned the corruption of the youth of Athens. And in Victorian England, Charles Dickens described graphically the young pickpockets and plug-uglies who preyed upon the respectable denizens of that very proper and prim isle in the sea.

No, juvenile delinquency and youthful criminality are not new ailments, but as far as we can ascertain, the ailment is more widespread and explosive today than ever before. A few facts are in order.

In the United States, in 1964, 37 per cent of all perpetrators of crimes were under 18 years of age. From 1957-65, the rate of delinquency rose 58 per cent to 1.2 million arrests and 697,000 court referrals. This was almost double the 32 per cent rise in juvenile population during the same period of time. Today, 2.5 million children (ages 10 to 17) have police records. Two of every 100 juveniles get into some trouble; almost 50 per cent of arrests made are of children; 1 of every 9 youngsters is in court before age eighteen.

In 1963, 45,800 children were living in public and voluntary institutions and camps. In New Jersey in 1965, almost 45 per cent of the prisoners were *under* twenty-one. . . .

To be sure, many police cases are merely traffic violations and ought not be considered delinquent acts. But there is much undetected or unreported delinquency, especially among the middle and upper economic classes. If the present trend continues, we are told, 3 to 4 million children will have been in court, and perhaps 20 per cent of all kids will have been in some scrape with the law by 1973.

America is not by any means the lone sufferer, or the worst offender. In fact, our juvenile delinquency rate of 1.8 per cent is lower than the rates of other nations. Sweden has the highest and fastest-growing rate—3 per cent. Japan's rate is 1.2, and is climbing faster than ours. Turkey and Israel have watched their rates double in a decade. England has its gangs and its Teddie Boys, and that worker's paradise that constitutes the Soviet Union is plagued by gangs and thugs, Marx and Lenin notwithstanding. Even France—where juvenile delinquency was relatively rare a decade ago—has contracted the disorder. The number of juveniles in prison leaped from 500 to 4,500 between 1956 and 1966. In 1956 the police handled 15,000 cases; in 1966 the figure soared to 45,000.

Clearly (and sorrowfully) juvenile delinquency is not a problem of America or the western world or capitalist nations alone. It is a world-wide problem and a universal malady.

What are the causes of juvenile delinquency?

Students of the subject differ on this matter. All agree that social upheavals and radical change in society are factors in the climbing rate of juvenile crime. War is one of the major factors: fathers are away; mothers and children often work; tensions mount; housing is inadequate and overcrowded; people migrate and are uprooted; schools are crowded and understaffed; violence and corruption have become the norm. But war and similar social upheavals are merely catalysts for more fundamental causes— causes that criminologists, psychologists, sociologists, social workers, and police officials have been trying to pinpoint. Whether delinquency is caused by psychological, sociological, ecological, or economic factors is hotly contested.

Some experts stress the environmental or ecological factors. Poor housing, poor recreational facilities, inferior education, lack of basic securities, poverty (especially amidst affluence) these are the factors that breed delinquency and crime, they tell us.

Poverty is obviously a factor in engendering delinquency. This is evident from the high incidence of delinquency found in the minority groups of deprived and exploited communities. In France, for example, nearly half the delinquents are from slum areas. The inordinately high rate of delinquency and crime among Puerto Ricans and Negroes is not due to any racial factor or genetic flaw; it is traceable to slums, lack of recreation, exploitation, lack of job opportunities, and grinding, traumatic, shattering *frustration*. As Professor Marvin E. Wolfgang of the University of Pennsylvania has shown: "Delinquency becomes both a protest against the social system that blocks the path to success, and a way, albeit illegitimate, to acquire recognition and status. . . ."

Poverty and slums alone do not make for delinquency, however. That is evident from the fact that some of the most affluent nations in the world have enormously dangerous rates of delinquency (*e.g.*, the United States, Sweden, West Germany, Japan, etc.).

In our own country, delinquency exists among the middle and upper economic classes. A study was made of seventeen middle-class delinquents from good Jewish homes in Queens. The boys had looted $100,000 in merchandise and money over a five-year period. These boys, who lacked for nothing, defended their actions by complaining that they "had nothing to do." "On Friday nights," they averred, "the leagues take over the bowling alleys and on weekends, especially Sunday mornings, the men take over the park." They decried the lack of thrills and excitement.

East Hampton, Long Island—one of America's most affluent resorts—was the scene of a narcotics raid in 1965. Three hundred young people were arrested; seventeen

were held over for criminal court. Why had these youngsters from rich homes gone wrong? They were seeking a
"bash" and "thrills," as they put it. Evidently, poverty is
not the only cause of crime.

Nor is capitalism the cause, Marx and Lenin notwithstanding. Communist theoreticians have argued that crime
is the offspring of socio-economic classes and conflicts.
Eliminate class distinctions, they averred, and you eliminate
crime and delinquency. But after a half-century of Red
rule, delinquency and crime still plague the "worker's Paradise."

Sociologists seek the answers in the realm of social conflicts and status deprivation. Albert Cohen and others, for
example, believe that juvenile delinquency among the poor
is an expression of status deprivation. Lower-class children
want, but can't achieve middle-class values and status because of the broad gap between the classes. Hence, they
value what the middle class rejects. They cheat and steal;
they take dope and flunk out of school; they dress in a
sloppy, outrageous fashion. Delinquents rebel against
middle-class norms and create a value system that seeks to
protect the individual from awareness of his lower-class
lack of esteem. The juvenile gang serves such a purpose; it
becomes the lower-class culture of the adolescent; it fur-
nishes criminal models and aberrant idols for the young to
emulate.

Herbert Bloch and Arthur Niederhoffer have suggested
another sociological cause for aggressive adolescent behavior and gangs. They see the pattern as a reflection of the
conflict between adolescent boys and an adult society that
refuses to let them play an adult role in the family, in employment, and in sex.

Psychologists look for causes in the mind and unconscious of man. Mental illness and emotional deprivation and conflict cause delinquency, they say.

A survey of American delinquents conducted by the Senate Subcommittee on Juvenile Delinquency seems to confirm this thesis. It found that one out of ten children in the five to seventeen age-group showed signs of odd behavior warranting treatment. The chairman, Senator Thomas J. Dodd, declared that "we reap our annual harvest of close to 600,000 delinquents from this emotionally disturbed group."

Not all psychologists, however, concur that delinquents are emotionally disturbed in the pathological sense. Dr. Erik Erikson, for example, considers the adolescent crisis as normal and unavoidable. "It is the crisis of the adolescent trying to determine what he is to *become;* it is his quest for 'ego identity.'" And Professor Irving Sarnoff writes that the "aggrandizement drive" is at the root of the matter. He urges that we create a new system of values and socioeconomics to eliminate the values that sow strife and antagonism.

One other view merits our attention. Several students of juvenile delinquency (notably Professors Negley Teeters, Jackson Toby, and William Kvaraceus) blame our school systems. They tell us that the school tries to be all things to all children. Since many children are not apt, bright, or interested, a million dropouts walk our streets. Kvaraceus urges a varied curriculum to meet the varied needs of all children. Others suggest an earlier legal drop-out age, with a compulsory work or apprenticeship program to replace the academic hours. Toby writes that we must grant recognition in school to the delinquent in order to satisfy his yearning for ego and status.

All of these factors, however, are ancillary ones; the

main problem seems to lie in other areas—namely, *the family*. In the words of Harry E. Barnes and Negley Teeters: "In the last analysis, lack of parental control and absence of parental insight provide the basis for delinquency and crime." And as J. Edgar Hoover observed: "Juvenile delinquency is a product of adult neglect."

Almost every expert in the field of juvenile delinquency agrees that the root of the problem can be traced to the home and family. True, slums, poverty, poor recreation, physical and psychological problems are factors in nurturing delinquents, but those same slums that bred murderers and thugs gave us judges and doctors. Clearly, another factor is determinative—and that factor is the family.

Striking evidence of the role of the family in delinquency has been produced by Harvard's great criminologists Sheldon and Eleanor Glueck. For many years those two eminent students of juvenile delinquency have attempted to unravel the causes of the disease and suggest means of arresting it. In fact, the Gluecks have devised a prediction table by which they assert they can predict a future delinquent while the subject is still an infant. The Gluecks claim 90 per cent accuracy for their prediction table. Their predictions are based on five domestic factors: 1) Father's discipline; 2) Mother's supervision; 3) Father's affection for son; 4) Mother's affection; 5) Cohesiveness of the family. The Glueck studies have proved that *inadequate family life* is the major factor leading to delinquency. Drunkenness, criminality, mental retardation, emotional disturbance, poor work habits, dependence on relief, low cultural levels, and emotional deprivation are the traits common to most proto-delinquent and delinquent families. With an adequate, wholesome family life, they write, there is only a 3 per cent chance of raising a delinquent child. In a strained, unwholesome home, there is a 98 per cent chance that a delinquent will be produced.

The Gluecks have received startling confirmation of this from other sources and studies. A New York City survey indicated that 1 per cent of the city's families produces over 75 per cent of the juvenile delinquents. In these sick families, 20.3 per cent of the fathers and 7.4 per cent of the mothers were alcoholics or junkies; 15.8 per cent of the mothers and 7 per cent of the fathers were mentally ill; 32 per cent of the mothers and 15 per cent of the fathers were cripples; 28 per cent of the fathers had deserted their families; 12 per cent of the mothers and 11 per cent of the fathers abused their children, and 15 per cent of the mothers were sexually immoral.

Various American studies of delinquency have shown that there is a high incidence of delinquency in broken homes. French studies have come to the same conclusion. Significantly, parental models and images have much to do with producing antisocial types. "The lack of a strong father image is central," writes sociologist Dr. James Thorpe. Unquestionably, the lack of a strong father image in the Puerto Rican and Negro family lies at the core of the high incidence of criminality in those deprived ethnic groups. Lacking a solid, wholesome parental image—an "idol" whom they can emulate—delinquent children turn to criminals in their search for "idols." They pattern themselves on the successful thug or hoodlum who drives a big car, wears fine, flashy clothes, and generally thumbs his nose at society.

Middle-class and upper-class delinquents are often bred by parents who set improper and criminal patterns. For example, a study by Norman Epstein at the North Shore Guidance Center on Long Island disclosed that affluent boys had learned criminality at home in seemingly harmless ways. Their fathers often taught the boys the tricks of the trades—shady deals, corrupt business and tax practices, etc. They frequently boasted to their boys of their illegal business dealings, truancy, sexual adventures, and shortcuts to success. Consequently, the boys became confused by conflicting precepts and examples. Their delinquency, unlike that of their poor counterparts, was not rebellion against the raw deal in life; it was caused by a corrupt, distorted parental image that was at variance with religious and societal norms. As Joseph M. Kennick, past President of the National Conference of Juvenile Agencies observed: "We spoil too many children and we make them grow up too soon. And we provide a paradox—we deceive, cheat, break the law, and expect them to be honest! We extenuate their guilt, and we fail to enforce the rules ourselves."

It is clear, painfully clear, that the root cause of delinquency lies not in the school, or society, or slum, or lack of recreation: it lies in the family, the home—the nuclear element of a civilization. And if parents fail, little can be done to rectify the damage.

The Jewish home has been exemplary throughout the ages. For this reason, perhaps more than any other, delinquency and criminality are extremely low in the Jewish group. For a long time American prison and crime statistics have borne out the fact that the Jewish crime rate is very low and that rare is the Jew who has committed a crime of violence.

This is true of delinquency as well. In over a decade of

rabbinical service in three communities I have encountered only two delinquent adolescents, and their infractions were minor. There are, unfortunately, few studies of delinquency among Jews. One such study, by Professor Sophie Robison, revealed that the rate among Jewish children in New York City is low and has been dropping. In 1930, for example, almost 20 per cent of court cases involved Jews, while the Jewish population of the city was about 30 per cent. One-third of those arrested, however, were charged merely with peddling or begging. In 1952, with Jews forming 27.2 per cent or so of the white population, the court cases dealing with Jews was an infinitesimal 3 per cent. Robison notes, however, that there are more Jewish adolescents arrested today than formerly for violent, aggressive acts. Still, the truth is that Jews can proudly point to a minute rate of delinquency and criminality.

Why? Of course, the Jewish community is fairly affluent. Its homes are pleasant; its recreational outlets abundant. But above all, the Jewish home has been marked by love and discipline, emotional stability and domestic peace. The Jewish family has always been a closely-knit, adhesive unit. This has not been accidental; it has been the result of centuries of external pressures, ghettos, pogroms, and hostility that turned the family inward to itself rather than outward to society. But more. The successful Jewish family unit is the product of generations of *religious conditioning and traditions*.

The Bible ordains that children honor and revere their parents. "Honor your father and mother" [1] declares the fifth commandment of the Decalogue. Leviticus uses somewhat different terminology: "A man shall fear his mother and his father." [2] The Talmudic sages offer some acute comments on filial piety and the concepts of honor and fear, or reverence. They note that the father is mentioned first in the Decalogue, while in Leviticus 19:3 the mother comes first. They point out that this is intentional on the part of the Lawgiver: Man normally reveres and fears his father most of all. Leviticus, therefore, seeks to balance the scale by placing the mother first, thus stressing that we must honor *both* parents equally. [3]

Wherein does "honor" differ from "fear?" This rabbinic insight is instructive:

> *To "fear" one's parents means that one should never sit in father's place, occupy his seat, contradict him or decide against him. To "honor" a parent means that one must present a parent food, drink, clothing, shelter, and assist him when he enters or leaves.* [4]

Parents were depicted as God's partners in fashioning a human being. [5] Consequently, one is to revere parents as much as one reveres the Lord. When a child does so, God's presence, so to speak, dwells among the people. [6] "Hearken unto your father that begot you, and despise not your mother when she is old," observed the authors of Proverbs, [7] for "God rewards in the next world those who honor their parents." [8]

In relating to parents, children were expected to show respect even if a parent had erred or sinned; they were to be diplomatic in correcting a wayward parent. [9] And significantly, they must exhibit the proper spirit in helping their parents, as this passage from the Palestinian Talmud indicates:

A man may feed his father on fattened chickens and inherit Hell, and another may put his father to treading the mill, and inherit Paradise. In the first case, a son gave his father fattened chickens to eat, and the father said, 'My son, where did you get these?' The son said, 'Old man, old man, eat and be still, for dogs eat and are still.' He inherits Hell. The other man grinds in his mill when an order comes for millers to grind for the government. The son says, 'Father, come and grind here instead of me. If any ill treatment should happen, better it befall me than you. . . .' This one inherits Paradise.[10]

Notwithstanding Judaism's emphatic trend toward filial piety, there were defiant, and disloyal, rebellious and contentious children. Deuteronomy 21:18-21 tells us: "If a man has a disloyal and defiant son, who does not heed his father or mother . . . his father and mother shall take hold of him and bring him out to the elders of his town at the public place of his community. They shall say to the elders of his town, 'This son of ours is disloyal and defiant; he does not heed us. He is a wastrel and a drunkard.' Thereupon the men of his town shall stone him to death. Thus you will sweep out evil from your midst: all Israel will hear and be afraid." And Exodus 21:17 ordains that "he who reviles his father or mother shall surely die." Evidently, juvenile delinquency existed in ancient Israel, and was viewed so seriously that capital punishment was prescribed for the youngster who cursed his parents, struck them, rebelled against their wishes, violated the laws of the Torah or the admonitions of the sages or judges, or caroused in a drunken or gluttonous fashion.

Judaism, however, was repelled by the notion of capital punishment. As a result, all sorts of legal fictions were proposed to annul the law in practice, if not in spirit. One teacher was moved to observe that "the law of the rebellious and contentious son never was observed in the past and never will be observed in the future." [11]

The fictions the Talmudic scholars devised are not only insightful, but also psychologically and sociologically modern.

> *"We deduce that a rebellious son is not guilty unless he had both father and mother," declared Rabbi Meir. Rabbi Judah stated: "If his mother was not worthy of the father, the lad is not judged a rebellious and contentious son."*

A third view suggests that the father may have been responsible for the child's behavior by marrying a woman for sheer sexual beauty rather than good character. Thus he "brought a Satan into his house" and caused his child to rebel.[12]

From the foregoing material we see that delinquency was viewed as a creature of parental neglect, mismating, and broken homes. And this is apparent, too, from the several Biblical tales of aberrant children. Abraham's son by his concubine, Hagar, was Ishmael. The lad was under his corrupt Egyptian mother's spell; he is depraved—a baleful influence on his half-brother Isaac—and he is addicted to idolatry, mayhem and murder. Abraham has no choice but to expel the delinquent lest he contaminate the entire household. Obviously this "son of Hagar the Egyptian" was never imbued with Abraham's morality, while Isaac, "the son of Abraham," reflects a sound upbringing and careful parental control.[13] To the sons of his other concubines Abraham gave "gifts;" [14] to his beloved Isaac he gave "everything he had" [15]—both material and spiritual bounties, sustenance, and moral guidance.

Much the same is true of Esau, the twin brother of Jacob. Isaac spoiled Esau, was blind to his failings, showed unconscionable favoritism toward him, and extenuated his sins. The results were nearly disastrous; the bloody hunter almost turned his bow against his brother Jacob.[16]

A third illustration of delinquent children in the Bible is found in the unhappy domestic life of King David. David was an overly-indulgent father who excused the sins of his sons and extenuated their guilt. And he paid a fierce price: his favorite Absalom seduced his father's concubines, rebelled against him, and almost killed him. After General Joab slew the traitor, David mourned his "Absalom, Absalom"—even to the point of blaming Joab![17] David's son Adonijah rebelled against David while he was on his deathbed; only the loyalty of Benayahu and the Prophet Nathan averted a successful coup d'état.[18]

These are not merely pious legends or fanciful fictions. Each story seeks to drive home the lesson that children must respect their parents, and parents must guide their children if delinquency is to be prevented. And the fact that Jews have maintained such an exemplary record is due to an ingrained tradition of filial piety.

It is also due, however, to a deeply-rooted tradition of parental obligations to children—of care, concern, control, and compassion. As the Talmud puts it: "A parent who can prevent his family from sinning and fails to do so, is punished for the sins of all." [19]

A parent had certain specific duties vis-à-vis the child. There must be love for a child—even more love than for a parent.[20] The parent must provide for a child's nourishment and welfare,[21] and should not show favoritism to one son over the other—for such favoritism merely engenders envy and hatred.[22] This is evidently the point in the story of Joseph and his brothers. Father Jacob favors his youngest son, Joseph. He buys him a "coat of many colors," and so arouses the enmity of the other brothers that they can't even talk peacefully to Joseph. In the end, tragedy results: Joseph is nearly killed and is finally sold as a slave to Egypt. And old Father Jacob—believing his dear son to be dead—bears his grief until the ultimate reconciliation, many years later.[23] Thus the inevitable result of parental favoritism!

One of the fundamental duties of a parent toward his child has always been education. The Bible stresses the commandment to "teach your son diligently"[24] the precepts of Torah, the rudiments of faith, and the moral life. "Train a child in the way he must go," observed the author of Proverbs 22:6, "and even when he is old he will not depart from it." The Jewish parent took this duty—this religious *mitzvah* of educating the young—very, very seriously. Both father and mother poured fundamental knowledge into boys and girls. The home became a veritable school; the table a university. Later on in Jewish history, the sages laid down the curriculum each father and mother was to teach the young and the duties incumbent upon a parent. These included circumcision, redemption of the first born, study of Torah and the Hebrew language, marriage at the proper age, training in a trade or profession, and (curiously) even swimming and politics.[25] With the establishment of public schools in the first post-Christian century, every parent was expected to enroll his child in school by the time he was five or six years old.[26]

The education of a child was by no means limited to Torah and morals, however. There was to be a practical side to it as well, as is evident in this statement of Rabbi Judah: "Whoever fails to teach his son a trade . . . it is as if he teaches him piracy!"[27] Nor was Mother free from tending to the educational needs of the young. "How do women acquire merit?" queries a Talmudic sage. "By sending their children to study Torah in the synagogue, and their husbands to learn in the academies."[28] Indeed, Mother was charged with nurturing the religious atmosphere of home and hearth. And proper companions were to be sought out for the young.

This long-standing tradition conditioned Jews to stress intellectual pursuits, education, professional training, and love of learning. In its sacred manifestation, it inspired the dream of a Jewish parent in days gone by to raise a child to be a scholar of Torah; in its secular development, it impelled every peddler and tailor to strive to make his son a professional man—doctor, dentist, lawyer, or accountant—no matter how great the sacrifice. And with this stress on education, we can readily appreciate why the leisure time of Jewish youngsters has been occupied with such activities as studies, schoolwork, and Hebrew School, rather than with gangs, poolrooms, and criminal acts. Professor Jackson Toby underscores this factor in preventing juvenile delinquency among Jews. He writes that Jews who are today's delinquents "do not have a Jewish cultural orientation." And he adds: "Perhaps American society can learn from its Jewish subculture that placing a high valuation upon intellectual achievement is an indirect approach to crime prevention."

There is a third duty to be exercised by every Jewish parent, and this has been, in my opinion, a bulwark against juvenile delinquency. The Jewish parent was to *discipline* a child—even to the point of using corporal punishment. "He that spares his rod hates his son; but he that loves him chastens him betimes." [29] The Book of Proverbs is a splendid manual of child rearing and pedagogy. It urges us: "Correct your son and he will give you rest; yea he will give delight to your soul." [30] And furthermore: "The rod and reproof give wisdom; but a child left to himself causes shame to his mother." [31] Only a firm hand inculcates respect for law and order and reverence for God and Torah. In a striking passage, the Midrash notes that the "delinquents" of the Bible—viz., Ishmael, Esau, Absalom, and Adonijah—were all the products of over-coddling fathers who failed to correct and discipline their aberrant sons and neglected their parental duties.[32]

To be sure, there were limits even on parental powers and discipline. A parent was not allowed to administer excessive corporal punishment [33] and was advised not to use such discipline on a grown youngster.[34] Nor could a parent himself execute a criminal child or rebellious son—as was the practice in ancient Greece or Rome; only the Sanhedrin had that power. A parent had the right to betroth a minor daughter, but she could repudiate such a betrothal at age twelve.[35] And furthermore, a parent could not order a child to violate the laws of God. Reverence for parents could not be invoked to vitiate reverence for God or His laws.[36] In sum, the Jewish parent was urged to strike the happy balance between love and fear, tenderness and discipline, gentleness and firmness. As this passage indicates: "Let your left hand push away the child and let your right hand draw him near." [37]

One other parental duty is worth noting. The Jewish parent was expected to set the proper image for a child to emulate. He was to be exemplary, as worthy of filial respect as possible. And this applied to both father and mother, for Judaism recognized the dual roles of parents and the need of the young for both father and mother. Judaism had little patience with absentee mothers, vanishing fathers, and defaulting parents. Both father and mother were expected to set a wholesome model, to be paradigms of honesty, integrity, piety, and morality on whom the children were to pattern their lives.

A popular Hebrew proverb runs: "The deed of the fathers is a model for the children." How aptly put! A parent who lies, cheats, steals, fornicates, and violates ritual and moral rules of Judaism and society can scarcely expect his children to do otherwise. "He who guides his sons and daughters in the straight and honest path . . . will receive the Biblical blessing of 'peace in your tent.'" [38] "A parent should not make a promise to a child and then renege; for he thereby teaches the child to lie." [39]

One superb illustration of the role of parental images in saving children from sin is derived from the life of Joseph. His employer's wife seeks to seduce him—and almost succeeds. At the last moment, however, he resists, and flees from her clutches, avoiding the heinous sin of adultery.[40] The Rabbis inform us that at the crucial moment, when

Joseph was about to succumb to temptation, the image (literally, "icon") of his father Jacob appeared to him and stopped him from sinning.[41]

In sum, then, juvenile delinquency in Jewish families has been a minute problem because of long centuries of religious traditions and ingrained attitudes and conditioning, all of which combined to develop strong, closely-knit family units, filial piety, devoted parents, and wholesome home lives. The Jewish family stressed the importance of education, constructive use of leisure, reverence for God's laws and man's laws, and obedience to the moral way. The Jewish parent was noted for concern and care, rather than casualness and carousing. The parental image was elevated to the highest, most exemplary level. The adulation of child for parent was reflected in the respect the child showed for parental ideals and law and order.

Does this mean that it was easy to raise Jewish children? Not at all. The sages frequently refer to the chore as "the *pain* of rearing children." [42] Do I imply that Jewish parents never failed? Of course not: we have already noted the failures of some of our Patriarchs and Biblical heroes. And the Passover Haggadah reminds us that there are "four types of sons—one wise, one wicked, one simple, and one who can't even ask the questions." Obviously, there *is no* sure method, no foolproof technique of avoiding delinquency and raising righteous progeny. We have, however, succeeded in large measure; we have brought forth decent children despite poverty and adversity; we have boasted of "children whose virtue brought honor to their fathers." [43] And thereby we have a lesson to teach modern society.

Certainly our society must tackle the problem vigorously. We must clean up the slums; give decent jobs to deprived minority groups; revise school curricula; build adequate recreational facilities; treat—rather than merely punish—the criminal; revise techniques of incarceration and probation; spend more money on crime prevention, and hire more and better personnel to work with youth.

These measures, however, merely strike at the peripheral causes; they fight the symptoms and fail to wrestle with the core issue. That core issue, that fundamental cause is, as it has always been, inadequate, unhappy, unwholesome home life. We are not going to unravel the juvenile delinquency problem until we build adequate family lives and healthy domestic atmospheres with clearly defined values and norms.

This is, I believe, Judaism's message on the matter. We have succeeded where others have failed; we have realized that "the father of the righteous will greatly rejoice, and he that begets a wise child will have joy in him." [44] We have unstintingly invested time, effort, discipline, love, education, and material resources. And we have, until our times, reaped rich dividends.

Can modern man learn from the Jewish family? He had better, if he is going to save his children and grandchildren, for, as the sages observed, these are not merely our "children," but our "builders"—the builders of the future generations and tomorrow's civilization.[45] Build through our children we must, if tomorrow is to be brighter than today.

NOTES

[1] Exodus 20:12; Deuteronomy 5:16
[2] Leviticus 19:3
[3] Kiddushin 30af.
[4] Sifra pp. 86b; Kiddushin 31b
[5] Kiddushin 30b
[6] Yer. Peah I, 1; 15d

7 Proverbs 23:22; cf. 1:8 and 15:5
8 M. Peah I, 1
9 Kiddushin 32a
10 Yer. Peah I, 1; 15c
11 Sanhedrin 71a. middle; Yer. Sanhedrin VIII, 7; 26b; Tosefta Sanhedrin XI, 2 and 3; Sifré Deuteronomy §218 and §219, p. 114a
12 Sifré Deuteronomy §219, p. 114a, bottom
13 Genesis 16 and 21
14 Genesis 25:6
15 Genesis 25:5
16 Genesis 27
17 II Samuel 13-19
18 I Kings 1, 2
19 Shabbat 54b
20 Sotah 49a
21 Ketubot 50a on Psalm 106:3
22 Shabbat 10b
23 Genesis 37
24 Deuteronomy 6 and 11
25 Mekilta I, 165f; Kiddushin 29a, 31b; Tosefta Kiddushin I:8; Sanhedrin 76a; Pesahim 49a

26 Avot V, 21; Baba Batra 21a
27 Kiddushin 29a
28 Berakhot 17a
29 Proverbs 13:24; 19:18; 23:13,14; 13:1
30 Proverbs 29:17
31 Proverbs 29:15
32 Exodus Rabbah I, 1
33 Gittin 6b
34 Moed Katan 17a
35 Kiddushin 41a
36 Sifra p. 87a on Leviticus 19:3
37 Sanhedrin 107b; Semakhot II, 6
38 Yevamot 62b on Job 5:24
39 Sukkah 46b and 56b
40 Genesis 39:7-12
41 Genesis Rabbah LXXXVII, 7
42 Sanhedrin 19b; Genesis Rabbah XX, 7, etc.
43 Tanhuma *Vayikra* §7, Vol. II, p. 3a
44 Proverbs 23:24f.
45 Berakhot 64a

IV

The Aging

"The days of our years are three score ten;
and if by reason of strength, four score."
                                    PSALMS 90:10

MANY are the blessings of modern science and medicine, and not the least of those blessings is longevity; today the average American male has a life expectancy of sixty-eight years, and the average female seventy-three years. At the turn of the century the figure was considerably lower: just a little over 40 years.

As a result of these great achievements in medicine, nutrition, hygiene, and sanitation, our aging population is increasing to the point where people over sixty-five are no longer the rarities they were a century ago.

In 1860, less than a million Americans were over sixty-five; in 1967, over 18 million achieved the magic number. By 1980, about 24.5 million—9 per cent of our population—will be over sixty-five.

From 1950-58, our total population increased 14.6 per cent, and the aged population went up by 23.3 per cent. About 15 per cent of our voters are over sixty-five. The number of people over sixty-five is increasing by eight hundred daily, thanks to modern medicine. It seems as if man's age-old prayer for long life and length of days had been answered, and the fountain of youth has become a reality. In fact, some physicians believe that by the year 2,000, a life span of one hundred years will not be impossible.

Yet, longevity is not an unmixed blessing. Science and medicine have created another of their customary paradoxes: they have added years to our life, but not life to our years; they have prolonged our days, but also our suffering; they have given us longer life spans, but have not taught us how to spend those extra years in health, in happiness, in physical comfort, in creative activity or in dignity. In a word, the modern world has conferred more years on its citizens—but has found their minds and bodies superfluous. And here lies the tragic irony, the ghastly and cruel paradox of longevity.

One of the worst problems facing older people is the health problem. The body and mind are machines, and like machines, they develop kinks and breakdowns with the passage of years. Each repair job is costly, each hospital stay ruinous. Prior to the passage of the Medicare Bill, the specter of illness haunted our senior citizens. For many, costly illnesses spelled financial ruin for them or their children. The anguish of diseases of old age, of senility, of chronic illnesses remains despite Congressional legislation. Over 5 per cent of our senior citizens are in institutions. Science, despite its new study of geriatrics and diseases of the aged, has not yet solved that thorny issue of health for the elders of the land.

Another problem that plagues older people is the question of security. Only 25 per cent of our senior citizens are employed; 32 per cent depend on help from the government or from children. Three-fourths of our citizens over 65 have an income of *under* $1,000. Even with welfare payments and Social Security, poverty lurks just beyond the gates of most older people. Welfare payments average a mere $78.51 a month, and Social Security payments can hardly be considered munificent.

There is an even greater evil: People over *forty* are finding it increasingly difficult to find employment. I have met with a number of desperate men in their forties and early fifties who are young and healthy and productive but are washed up, finished, unwanted in the world of business. Imagine—not sixty-five but forty-five, and already too old for America's labor market and business world!

The older citizen has domestic difficulties and sociopsychological traumas as well: How to carry on after losing one's mate? Where to live? With children? With *which* children? In an institution? How to make friends in shifting urban areas whose population changes radically? How to find companionship in suburbia, where children are pre-occupied, grandchildren are busy, and older folks are few and far between? How to overcome the sense of loneliness and ennui; of futility and boredom? No job. No companions. No useful tasks. No creative activity. No *raison d'être*. Children squabbling over their filial duties. Unwanted. In the way. A burden to others. Unable to care for oneself. . . .

There is yet another shame attendant upon old age—at least in America. Youth deprecates old age; young people poo-poo the wisdom and ability of the hoary heads. As George Chapman put it: "Young men think old men are fools; but old men *know* young men are fools."

"What do you old folks know?" seems to have become the motto of a nation of youth worshippers. Is it any wonder that most elderly people feel superfluous and rejected? Is it any surprise that many long for death rather than a life of insecurity, of illness, of loneliness, of charity, of family friction, of condescension?

The American mentality is compounding the problem. Ours is a youthful civilization; it reveres youth, it worships adolescence, it is child-centered.

A number of factors have created this phenomenon. For one thing, Americans seem to have a morbid fear of growing old, of maturing, of developing a gray hair. Beauty parlors do booming businesses on men and women in a feverish attempt to obliterate all shades of gray, wrinkles, furrows, and other telltale signs of advancing years. The most revolting radio and television commercials assure unwanted wives and unpopular husbands that gray hairs are at the root of the matter: just tint your hair and he'll ask you to dance once again; she'll embrace you once more. . . .

This morbid fear of aging (and, incidentally, of death) has given birth to a new vocabulary of euphemisms. A woman's age is a better-kept secret than America's missile defense. We do not speak of old age; we talk of "golden years." We do not build old-age homes; we erect "senior-citizen's residences." We do not organize old-age groups; we create "golden-age clubs." The subject of old age is taboo in America. We talk around it, never of it or to it.

Professor Abraham J. Heschel addressed a White House Conference on Aging in 1961 and offered the following keen diagnosis of our malady:

The typical attitude to old age is characterized by fear, confusion, absurdity, self-deception, and dishonesty. It is painful and bizarre. Old age is something we are all anxious to attain. However, once attained, we consider it a defeat, a form of capital punishment. Enabling us to reach old age, medical science may think, it gave us a blessing; however, we continue to act as if it were a disease. More money is spent on receiving cures and treatments of old age than on research on heart disease or cancer. You find more patients in the beauty parlors than in the hospitals. We would rather be bald than gray. A white hair is an abomination. Being old is a defeat, something to be ashamed of. Consequently, the authenticity and honesty of existence are readily exchanged for false lustre, for camouflage, sham, and deception.

A gray hair may destroy the chance for promotion, may cost a salesman his job and inwardly alienate a son from his father. The fear of being considered old has become a traumatic obsession. Only very few people are endowed with the rare and supreme courage to admit their true age without embarrassment. With the rest of us, courage and honesty go underground when the question of age is discussed. The most delightful resolution this Conference could pass would be to eliminate from now on any mention of the date of birth from the birth certificate.

Our dread of facing old age has destroyed our will to prepare for it. Psychology teaches us the principle of "repression." Man represses painful thoughts and experiences into his unconscious; he refuses to face reality and seeks to gloss over the unpleasant. But he has no true rest or peace of mind; the repressed unpleasantness of life haunts him, pains him, and disturbs him.

So too, we Americans seek to repress our concern over aging—but to no avail. The idea bothers us, haunts us, pains us. And worse: it paralyzes our desire to prepare for aging. We have no appreciation of what it means to be retired; we do not develop hobbies; we waste our precious leisure. Psychologically, we are completely unequipped for retirement and old age. Is it any surprise that so many older folks deteriorate mentally and physically when the cocoon of retirement and leisure envelopes them?

There is still another pathetic result of our "cult of youth." Because we worship youth, we waste maturity. We refuse to employ older workers and middle-aged executives. We impose foolish retirement ages in the army, in universities, in corporations, and in industries. We seem to believe that at sixty a man is useless, a dried-out lemon to be discarded out-of-hand. As a result, we are shamefully wasting brains and talent.

Walter Reuther once described old age as a time when we are "too old to work and too young to die," but this is simply not true. Many studies have found that men and women *can* be creative and productive in their sixties and seventies. James P. Mitchell, Secretary of Labor in the Eisenhower administration, issued a report demonstrating that older workers can produce just as well as younger ones, and that they are just as reliable and just as ambitious.

Secretary Mitchell concluded that "ability is ageless." How true! And how necessary it is for Americans to end *age* discrimination, which is every bit as vicious and immoral as racial and religious discrimination! Age should not be a major criterion for employment.

How many people have created great things in their advanced years! Adenauer, Churchill, De Gaulle, and Ben Gurion led their countries at an age when most men are dead and buried. George Bernard Shaw was still writing in his nineties, while Verdi created his *Otello* and *Falstaff* at the ages of seventy-four and eighty respectively. Toscanini was conducting in his eighties, and Grandma Moses became a painter when most are retired. Pope John XXIII ascended the Vatican throne when in his seventy-eighth year and became the most dynamic pontiff in centuries. And Professor Mordecai M. Kaplan is as challenging and stimulating as ever, even though he is an octogenarian. There is a school of law in California that hires retired law professors from all over the nation. This school has gathered a most distinguished law faculty of scholars who were thought to be too feeble and senile to create or to teach. Brainpower, however, is not necessarily curtailed by advancing years, and the California Law School boasts one of the great teaching staffs in the nation.

In sum, then, there are those who are old and uncreative at thirty-five, and others who are fresh and creative in their seventies. As Justice Oliver Wendel Holmes put it: "To be seventy years *young* is sometimes more cheerful and hopeful than to be forty years *old*." It is time for Americans to understand that old age is not a curse, not a misfortune, not a disease. It is time to revise our entire outlook on the meaning of the golden years.

Oriental cultures tend to revere the aged far more than do occidental cultures. Judaism, too, developed a deep reverence for the aged and a concern for their welfare. The blessing of old age (*arikhat yamim*) was one for which all Jews prayed and still pray to this day. In the Bible, the Patriarchs were rewarded by God for their piety with "old age, sated and full." There was no shame in discussing one's age; in fact when Jacob is queried by Pharaoh on the point, he answers forthrightly and frankly: "The days of my years are one-hundred-thirty." [1] Moses is reputed to have achieved the proverbial one-hundred and twenty years, and for all that "his eye was not dimmed, his spirit was not diminished." [2]

Ideally, every person hoped to achieve three score and ten years; and if by strength, perhaps even four score.[3] Our sages expanded on the ideal, reminding us that at sixty, one was "old;" at seventy, one was blessed with a "hoary head;" at eighty, one reached true "strength." [4]

Longevity was thought to be the reward for piety and moral living. The Bible informs us of this, for example, in exhorting us to "honor your father and mother," [5] and in the commandment to set the mother bird free from the nest when taking the eggs.[6] The sages also promised long life to the peacemakers.[7] In general, Judaism taught, "If you will surely harken to my commandments" and serve God and walk in his ways, then "your days and the days of your children will be lengthened on earth." [8]

We did not consider signs of advancing years to be omens of evil or harbingers of woe. Unlike the modern American, the Hebrew did not view gray hair as an affliction. "A crown of beauty," declare the Proverbs, "is the hoary head." [9] Wrote the rabbis, "The beauty of one's

face is a full beard." [10] Rabbi Eleazar ben Azariah was
elected to the Presidency of the Sanhedrin at the youthful
age of seventeen. He was overawed and fearful: How
could his older colleagues respect such a juvenile President?
So Eleazar prayed for a miracle. And lo and behold! overnight a miracle occurred; God whitened his hair and beard.
Eleazar was overjoyed. Now he looked like a sage!

To be sure, the reader must not get the impression that
the Hebrews saw no shortcomings in advanced years and
no problems in growing old. In Chapter 12 of his poignant
Allegory on Old Age, Koheleth wrote movingly of the
decline of body and mind that marks the advanced years of
life. He described in graphic and touching terms the "evil
days" when "the watchmen of the house tremble, and the
strong men are bent. . . . When one fears to climb a
height, and terrors lurk in a walk. . . . And the silver cord
is severed, and the golden bowl is shattered. . . ."

We understood that it is best to study when young,
when one's mind is like a *tabula rasa.*[11] We knew the physical problems that attend upon declining years. Rabbi
Simeon ben Eleazar interpreted Koheleth 12:1 as follows:
" 'Evil days'—this refers to the days of old age!" [12] We
shared with other cultures the gnawing fear of poverty,
illness, and abandonment in old age. Hence, the beautiful
Psalm 71: 9, "Cast me not off in old age; do not forsake me
when my strength fails." This Psalm is recited on the Jewish High Holy Days; it never fails to evoke tears and sobs
from the faithful.

Despite our apprehensions over the problems created by
old age, we recognized the value of maturity. Jewish tradition equated age with wisdom and youth with folly. The
Talmudic sages play on the Hebrew word for "elder"

(*zaken*) and tell us it is an acronym for "one who acquires wisdom." [13] So it was with all Eastern Cultures who viewed with alarm the brash young upstarts who sought to control nations and formulate philosophies. Judaism was no different: Its prophets and sages were distressed that young fools were running their nation.[14] Its view was simple: There is no teacher like experience, and no wisdom like maturation.[15]

Our civilization did not hold the view that age means debilitation of the mind and senility of the intellect. "The older a scholar becomes," states Talmud, "the wiser he becomes. Not so the ignoramus!" [16] Rabbi Simeon ben Eleazar (who seems to have been preoccupied with matters of gerontology) declared that "when older people and sages seem to be destroying, they really are building; when young fools seem to be building, they are really destroying." [17] One of the more emphatic passages is found in the Midrash and reads, "Honor your elders, for all of Israel is sustained because of them. For whoever takes counsel with his elders does not come to grief." [18]

Consequently, the Jewish community sought its leadership from the old—not the young—citizens. We have already noted the problems that beset the youthful Eleazar ben Azariah. The general rule was that the members of the Sanhedrin had to be bearded (*i.e.*, mature) before they could be elected.[19] Elsewhere we are informed that only mature people could serve as precentors, cantors, teachers, etc.[20]

"Rise before the hoary head, and revere the elder." [21] This magnificent verse set the tone for the reverential relationship that was to prevail between young and old, youth and elders. It is noteworthy that the sages hotly contested the meaning of this law.

Rabbi Meir would rise even in the presence of an old ignoramus, for he reasoned that some merit must have earned the man the gift of long life.[22]

Rabbi Jose, however, would only rise before an old scholar.

Issi ben Judah was of the opinion that the injunction included all elders—scholars and ignoramuses, saints and boors.

Rabbi Yohanan declared the law to be in accordance with Issi. And he expanded it to include non-Jewish old folks as well.

"What does it mean 'honor the elder'? It means we rise in his presence, we do not sit in his seat, or speak before he has spoken, or contradict him. And should you be tempted to shut your eyes and pretend not to see an old person, remember that the verse concludes: 'you shall revere the Lord.' This law is given over to man's heart and conscience; he may not ignore it." [23]

Insolence to elders was considered a heinous offense. One tradition tells us that Aaron's sons, Nadav and Avihu, were killed by God because they demeaned Moses and Aaron and prayed, "When will these two old ones die!" [24] Elders had a special amount of dignity. Hence, they were not required to perform commandments that might degrade them, such as aiding a stricken animal.[25] And anyone who insulted an older person had to pay a commensurate fine. A most beautiful teaching is that we are to respect an old scholar who has forgotten his learning; for he is like the broken tablets of the Ten Commandments lying in the Holy Ark.[26]

"When the young insult the old, when elders rise before youths," say the rabbis with unfeigned horror, "we will be in the era of the birth pangs of the Messiah and salvation will be near." [27] In sum, "he who greets an older person with reverence, it is as if he has greeted the Divine Presence." [28]

This stress on respect for elders led to a solicitude for old folks that was almost unparalleled among ancient civilizations. In some communities, elders were killed outright; in others (such as Sparta), they were exposed to the elements to perish; for some, suicide was the only recourse.

The Jew, however, insisted that children care for their aged loved ones. When that became impossible for physical or financial reasons, the aged were sent to an old-age home (*moshav zekenim*)—truly one of the unique creations of medieval and modern Jewry. We are used to the idea of a home for the aged in twentieth-century America; but who can believe that five or six centuries ago, Italy, Poland, Germany, and other lands boasted of such institutions for Jewish senior citizens?

The Jewish tradition grasped the idea of creative retirement for the aged long ago. We are informed in the Book of Numbers [29] that the Levites were to retire from their work in the Sanctuary (later on, in the Temple of Jerusalem) once they reached their fiftieth year. But they were expected to continue to "serve their brethren in the tent of meeting." This ambiguous passage is explained by the sages in a most instructive way: "The retired Levite continues to do light work such as closing the Temple gates, singing in the choir, and loading the wagons." [30] In other words, some form of creative activity was believed essential for the well being of retired individuals. As Dr. Heschel puts it: "To be retired is not to be retarded!" Upon visiting the Jewish home for the aged, in years gone by, one was struck by the fact that many elderly gentlemen were engaged in intellectual activities. Torah study was the delight of their retirement. Men who had longed for leisure time in which to study Talmud, to pore over the Bible, to delve into the mysteries of Kabbalah, were free at last to indulge in their hoped-for pastime and cherished avocation. I myself remember the scene in the *Bet Ha-Midrash* (study hall) of one of the famous homes for the aged: the hall was crowded with elderly students, its walls resounded with the din of Torah. They were not bored; their minds were not vegetating; they found meaning to their older years. As Rabbi Nehorai had observed ages ago: "Torah—unlike trades—gives a person a future, and hope in his old age." [31]

I wonder whether this will be possible now that Torah study is neglected and ignorance is rife? How, indeed, will our present generation of Jews find the intellectual stimulation of Torah in their declining years when they cannot even grasp the basics of Jewish Knowledge?

Although we stressed solicitude and care for the elderly and honor for the aged, we perceived that the aged, too, have a responsibility to the society. They have no right to impose on others unfairly and improperly or become nuisances. Rabbi Simeon ben Eleazar (who, we have seen, had a deep concern for the aged) taught: "How do we know that an older person has no right to impose unnecessarily and trouble people unfairly? From the verse in Leviticus 19:32, '. . . elder, and *you* shall fear your God, I am the Lord.'" [32] Likewise, workers in danger of losing money by rising in the presence of their elders need not do so. There are, then, limits on the privileges of the aged who may not exploit their status for selfish purposes and unfair advantage.

Most important of all, the Jewish people maintained a

wholesome attitude to life, to aging, and to death. We knew the beauty of youth, and the delights of savoring each day to the fullest. Koheleth urged, "Enjoy, young man, your youth" and the Psalmist prayed to God to "teach us to number our days wisely." The fullest enjoyment of each precious moment, of each delicious experience, of each blessed hour God has bestowed upon us—this was the spirit of Jewish living. The late James T. Shotwell, who was active until his ninety-first year, summed up this attitude in one of his poems:

> *Time is a cunning thief, beware,*
> *He picks our pockets daily,*
> *Not an old graybeard, bent with care*
> *But a youngster grinning gaily,*
> *The glass and scythe are mere disguise,*
> *To cover his queer behavings,*
> *And you find at last with sudden surprise,*
> *He has stolen all your savings.*
> *But when this happens the thing to do*
> *Is not to beg or borrow,*
> *But with defter fingers rifle him too,*
> *And steal another tomorrow.*

We faced the matter of aging with courage and equanimity, for we knew that elders enjoyed a position of honor in the community, and we remembered that some of our folk heroes had reached great heights in their middle or even later years. Had not Moses written his greatest songs close to his death? Had not Rabbi Akivah turned to study Torah when already a mature man?

Nor were we afraid of death. As the Psalmist sang:

"Though I walk through the valley of the shadow of death I will fear no evil, for Thou art with me." "Prepare yourself," taught Rabbi Jacob, "to meet your Maker. For this world is merely a corridor leading to the palace of eternal life." Death held less terror for a people filled with the idea that a greater, more blissful world lay just ahead in the world of tomorrow.

The ancient Spartans were brutes, but they were honest. They exposed their useless old folks to the elements and killed them. We are more civilized; we deposit them in stinking nursing homes and in remote old folks homes so that they are out of sight and mind. We turn them into useless hulks of once-proud people. We strip them of their honor, their dignity, their usefulness. We utilize money and brains and surgical skills in order to keep them alive. And then we kill them each day, each hour, by reducing them to rubble.

The time has come, I believe, for us to face the question of the aging fairly and squarely. Justice demands it.

The time has come, I believe, to revise our own attitudes towards aging. Truth requires it.

The time has come, I believe, for us to change our orientation and realize that youth is not the only blessed time of life. Morality calls for it.

I am suggesting simply this:

Respect and revere our elders;

Keep them useful and productive;

Prepare our own attitudes for the golden years.

How many beauteous blessings are stored up for us! How many sweet, serene hours can be ours if we but recognize that old age can be our golden years!

Remember the words of Robert Browning?

Grow old with me, the best is yet to be,
The last of life for which the first was made.

NOTES

1 Genesis 47:8
2 Deuteronomy 34:7
3 Psalm 90:10
4 Avot V, 21; Baba Batra 75a; Yer. Bikkurim I, 1; 64c
5 Exodus 20:12
6 Deuteronomy 22:6f.
7 Sifré Deuteronomy § 336, p. 141a, on Isaiah 54:13
8 Deuteronomy 11:13-21
9 Proverbs 16:31; cf. 20:29
10 Shabbat 152a
11 Avot IV, 20
12 Shabbat 151bf.
13 Sifra, end of chapter 7, p. 91a; Kiddushin 32b
14 Cf. Isaiah 3:12, 9:14; Koheleth 10:16
15 Proverbs 7:7, 22:14; Job 32:4-7; Ben Sira 8:8 ff, 25:4 ff.
16 Shabbat 152a on Job 12:12, 20; cf. Kinim III, 6
17 Tosefta Avodah Zorah I, 3; Megillah 31b
18 Exodus Rabbah III, 8 and V, 12;
cf. Sifré on Deuteronomy 32:7, § 310, p. 134a
19 Sanhedrin 17a; Baba Batra 120a
20 Tosefta Hagiga I, 4
21 Leviticus 19:32
22 Yer. Bikkurim III, 3; 65c, near the bottom.
23 Sifra, Chapter 7, end, p. 91a; Kiddushin 32b-33b; Yer. Bikkurim III, 3; 65c middle
24 Sanhedrin 52a; cf. Makkot 10a
25 Berakhot 19b on Deuteronomy 22:1
26 Berakhot 8b; Yer. Moed Katan III, 1; p. 81d bottom
27 Sotah 49b
28 Genesis Rabbah LXXXIII, 6, end
29 Numbers 8:24-26
30 Sifré Numbers § 63, p. 16b; cf. Rashi and Ramban *ad loc.*
31 Kiddushin 82a and b on Isaiah 40:31 and Psalm 92:15
32 Sifra, end of chapter 7, p. 91a; Yer. Bikkurim III, 3; 65c middle

V

Leisure Time—
Blessing or Curse?

"Six days shall you labor and do all your work."
EXODUS 20:9

FIFTY years ago, the average worker put in a fifty-hour week with one day of rest. Women and children slaved in stinking sweat shops and fetid mines. In 1963 the average worker was on the job forty-one hours; many enjoyed a week-end Sabbath. Today, the labor unions are seriously urging a thirty-two-hour week, and some trades are actually working on such a reduced schedule.

President Lyndon B. Johnson observed in his inaugural address (January 20, 1965) that "ours is a time of change—rapid and fantastic change . . . shaking old values and uprooting old ways." It is apparent that his analysis is true in the realm of work and leisure. The Fourth Commandment reads: "Remember the Sabbath Day and keep it holy; six days shall you labor and do all your work. But you shall rest on the seventh day because it is holy." This injunction has evidently been altered radically to read *not* six days of

79

labor, not even five—but now four days and potentially less!

Why the radical change in the American concept of a work week? Of course, modern man craves more leisure, more time off, more freedom from the daily routine. But the basic answer is the chronic unemployment of the American labor force, a figure that fluctuates between three and four million even in prosperous times. Our nation's unemployment problem seems to be due to several factors. First, is the matter of automation. Today machines are taking over the work of dozens, even hundreds of men. It is suggested that by the next twenty-five years, *2 per cent* of the population could produce all of our nation's needs!

Second, our population is increasing: one million workers join the labor force each year. But only 33,000 new jobs are created yearly to meet these swelling needs.

Finally, the masses are receiving more and better education, and therefore we are producing more skilled workers and have less and less need for non-skilled laborers, who find themselves unable to obtain even the most menial employment. In other words, the high school drop-outs are trapped in a dead end, unable to find jobs and unprepared to earn a decent living. This group constitutes one of the largest bodies of unemployed in our land.

Organized labor, consequently, has been urging shorter work weeks and work days in order to take up the slack of unemployment. Surprisingly enough, there are serious proponents of shorter work days and work weeks from ranks other than that of labor. Their arguments follow this pattern: the shorter work week is good because it means more money for less work; in turn, the workers will enjoy more leisure, during which they will spend their wages. (The idea is that workers will prime the pump of American prosperity by spending their wages during leisure periods.) More leisure means more hobbies and recreation; each worker will be able to relax, to engage in sports, to travel, to enjoy the good things in life. In addition, the new leisure class will have greater opportunities for education and culture. They will become the new habitués of museums and concert halls; they will read books, and paint, and play the piano. In short, greater leisure will produce a whole new generation of *illuminati.*

Not all observers of the contemporary scene are as sanguine about the blessings of leisure time. In fact, the opponents of the shorter work week are even more convincing, in my judgment, than the proponents. They maintain that inflation is certain to be spurred on by less work and more money. They tell us that "moonlighting" will increase, and people will fill their greater leisure with additional jobs. Today it is estimated that three-and-a-half million Americans hold down second and even third jobs: Imagine what will happen if we institute a four-day week!

There is a very severe practical problem engendered by shorter work weeks. In the race to the moon, in the battle with the Soviets for world leadership, in the contest for military superiority, can we produce enough on thirty-hour weeks? In 1957, the then Senator Lyndon B. Johnson said no: we cannot produce enough missiles for our defense needs on a reduced work schedule. But today, the views seem to have changed. . . .

Greater leisure has created a philosophical and psychological dilemma. That dilemma can be summarized in one word—*boredom*. If workers are bored today, I shudder to contemplate the extent of ennui in the year 2,000 when we will enjoy 660 billion more leisure hours than in 1950. Many psychiatrists find a greater incidence of breakdowns and suicides on weekends when the blessings of leisure hours are supposed to be manifest. And many retired workers and professionals complain that leisure and retirement are *not* unmixed blessings. Some bemoan these "honey-do" years, when all the husband hears is strident demands of his wife who exhorts: "Honey, do this! Honey, do that!" Often retired people deteriorate physically and mentally due to too much time on their hands without a *raison d'être*. I have known people who worked well into their eighties with no apparent ill effects. But when well-intentioned relatives retired these workers, when the American retirement system put them out to pasture, boredom, emptiness, mental and physical decline—even death—set in.

Unfortunately, greater leisure and early retirement are the portion of those least prepared for it and least capable of enjoying it to the utmost. The worker trained to run a lathe or drive a truck, who has no hobbies, no cultural interests, no avocations, vegetates when shelved. As Professor Arthur Schlesinger Jr. put it: "The most dangerous threat hanging over American Society is the threat of leisure . . . and those who have the least preparation for it will have the most of it." Professor Isaac Asimov, scientist and science fiction writer, comes to the same conclusion. In looking forward to the Utopia of the year 2014, he foresees the following:

> *Mankind will suffer badly from the disease of boredom, a disease spreading more widely each year and*

growing in intensity. This will have serious mental, emotional, and sociological consequences. . . .

*Indeed, the most somber speculation I can make about A.D. 2014 is that in a society of enforced leisure, the most glorious single word in the vocabulary will have become—*work!

In short, the brave new worlds of which Aldous Huxley writes, and the great, big, beautiful tomorrow extolled in blaring cacaphony at the New York World's Fair of 1964-65 are perhaps not so brave and not so beautiful. It is not clear at all whether increased leisure time will be a blessing or a curse.

In contradistinction to the modern deprecation of work and exaltation of leisure, Judaism teaches that work is one of the most precious elements in life.

For example, Jewish tradition never viewed work as a curse; on the contrary—it exalts labor and extols creative occupations. God placed Adam in the Garden of Eden "to work it and to protect it." [1] In other words, man's idyllic state was not that of a lazy wastrel who lived off God's largesse; even in Eden, in his state of Paradise, man was expected to do some labor. Legend has it that when Adam was expelled from Eden and was consigned to "labor with the sweat of your brow," he began to weep. "Am I to eat of the same food in the same trough as my beast?" he cried. "No," said God, "for you and only you shall eat bread as the fruit of your labor."

Rhapsodically does the Psalmist sing of the joys of labor: "When you eat the labor of your hands, happy shall you be, and it will be well with you." [2] It is no coincidence that the great figures of the Bible engaged in work—some of it menial by today's standards. Thus we read that Moses was a shepherd, as were Saul and David; Elisha was a farmer, and Amos a herdsman and tender of sycamore trees.

Shemayia urged man to "love work," [3] and other sages reminded us that we should combine Torah study with a worldly occupation, for "if there is no flour there can be no Torah."

Moreover, the Jewish tradition taught that labor is a *mitzvah*—a Divine imperative. Some of the sages considered the Fourth Commandment to be not just a negative precept to abstain from work on the Sabbath but a positive injunction to labor: "Six days shall you *labor*." [4] For this reason, the Talmudic sages earned their living in every conceivable fashion: some were blacksmiths, some sandal makers, some shepherds, and some merchants. No task was too menial, nor was any honest occupation too humble for titans like Rabbi Akivah, Rabbi Joshua ben Hananiah, Rabbi Yohanan, Rabbi Yose, and hundreds of others. These men truly believed that "work brings honor to the worker." [5] And they were sincere when they urged a person to "work at any trade—even one strange to him—rather than depend on charity." [6]

The Jewish People maintained a kind of "Puritan ethic" which molded their way of life—glorifying industriousness while denigrating idleness. The Book of Proverbs is replete with passages extolling the virtue of hard work, while denouncing the folly of indolence. "Go to the ant, you sluggard," urges the author of Proverbs 6:6 as he admonishes man to take a lesson from that toiling little creature. "Sweet is the sleep of the worker" [7] wrote Koheleth while denouncing the life of the idle—and corrupt—rich.

"Greater is the person who benefits from the work of his

hands," declared the third-century Rabbi, Ulla, "than he who fears God." [8] Elsewhere, Rabbi Jacob teaches that God does not bless the works of our hands when we are idle; rather, He blesses the works of our hands when we are industrious and occupied in constructive labor.[9] So obnoxious was the slothful person that Rabbi Yose, Rabbi Meir and Rabbi Judah (second century C.E.) declared: "He who does not engage in some occupation brings death upon himself!" [10]

To be sure, there were some scholars like Rabbi Simeon bar Yohai (second century C.E.) who deprecated worldly occupations and urged his followers to study Torah day and night. It is related that once he left a cave where he had been clandestinely studying Torah with his son (Emperor Hadrian had forbidden the study of Torah on penalty of death) when he came upon a farmer plowing the field. Angered by the sight of a Jew "neglecting the Eternal Life" in order to pursue the needs of the "temporal life," he cast an evil eye on the farmer and incinerated him, along with his field and ox. Whereupon a celestial voice came from heaven and ordered Simeon to return to his cave and cease from destroying God's world. Simeon was clearly in a tiny minority; his other-worldly philosophy that negated this world and deprecated manual labor was rejected by Jewish tradition.[11]

Assuredly, there were those who preferred study and contemplation, prayer and pietism to worldly occupations. In the middle ages and early modern times, this trend sharpened in response to external persecutions and oppressions. But let us recall the great figures of Jewish learning and the lives they led: Saadiah Gaon was a physician, as were Judah Halevi and Moses Maimonides, and a host of other greats; Rashi was a vintner; Rabbi Isaac Lampronti earned his living as a dancing teacher! In fact, for centuries rabbis resisted becoming paid professionals. Were it not for economic pressures and inordinate demands on their time, I believe the rabbis of today would still be self sufficient, choosing to earn their livelihoods from secular pursuits while serving the Jewish community gratis.

And there is yet another teaching of Jewish tradition to bear in mind: We Jews knew what to do with our leisure and how to make the most of it. We abhorred *batlanut* (time wasting) and had contempt for *batlanim* (wastrels, vagrants) who had no permanent means of earning a livelihood. Some synagogues, even in our own day, would lure these men of leisure for sacred tasks such as providing a *minyan* (quorum) for prayers and devoting themselves to the study of Talmud. Even a rich person was expected to do something creative with his leisure, and the Talmud exhorted the wealthiest matron to keep busy with sewing or some other work.[12]

We know the character of the Jewish people from the way we spent our leisure in days gone by. We enjoyed our leisure by rediscovering the beauty of family life. We exploited our leisure by turning to the synagogue for prayer. We capitalized on our leisure by studying Torah in the belief that the pursuit of knowledge and the imbibing of God's life-giving waters are the *summmum bonum* of life and a foretaste of Paradise.

Greater leisure time poses greater challenges to man than he had anticipated. Is this new phenomenon to be a blessing? Or a curse? It all depends on what use we make of it. We ought to bear in mind the way in which Judaism exploited free time for spiritual, cultural, and emotional enrichment. And we ought to ponder over the three terms we use most commonly to describe free time.

The first—"leisure"—is from the Old French word meaning "permission." Leisure permits us to do what we have always wanted to do; it frees us from the daily routine and the confines and shackles of our mundane existence.

The second term is "vacation" which comes from the Latin meaning "empty out." Leisure is a time to empty our minds and hearts of care and worry. It is an opportunity for refreshment—physical and spiritual, emotional and intellectual.

The third expression is "recreation," and it means to "re-create." Leisure implies the re-creation of old ties, the rekindling of love's flame, the recharging of spiritual batteries. Leisure should be utilized to rediscover life and its higher joys and pervasive divinity and sanctity. Television and golf, cards and Mah-jong, cha-cha and liquor may be pleasant and even necessary diversions, but they are not the means to enriching life. Long after man becomes jaded and sated with these vapid and feckless frivolities, he will still find fulfillment, satisfaction and enrichment in prayer and study, in love and family, in music and art, in the matters of the spirit and the creations of the mind.

By all means, then, let man prepare for the fuller enjoyment of the silver hours and golden years modern science and technology have given him. But let man evaluate this new-found Sabbath of life as God's gift, to be used accordingly and to be cherished appropriately.

NOTES

1 Genesis 2:15: Genesis Rabbah XVI, 5
2 Psalm 128:2
3 Avot I, 10
4 Avot de Rabbi Nathan, Version B, 21, p. 22b, ed. Schechter
5 Nedarim 49b
6 Baba Batra 110a
7 Koheleth 5:11
8 Berakhot 8a
9 Midrash Psalms, p. 99b § 3 on Psalm 23:1
10 Avot de Rabbi Nathan, Version B, 21, p. 22b
11 Shabbat 33b
12 Ketubot V, 5; 59b-62a

VI

Capital Punishment

*"A life for a life, an eye for an eye,
a tooth for a tooth. . . ."*

EXODUS 21:23 and 24

THE twenty-one men seated twenty feet and three doors away from Sing Sing's electrocution chamber had a close brush with death, but the New York State Legislature acted, and plucked the condemned men from the jaws of Hell—in some cases at the very last moment. On June 1, 1965, New York became the twelfth State in the Union to abolish capital punishment except in instances where a policeman is killed in the line of duty, or a prison guard is murdered by an escaping convict under life sentence.

Why had New York chosen to move toward abolition of the death penalty? The answer lies in the Whitmore Case. A poor drifter named George Whitmore Jr. was almost executed for a double murder he did *not* commit. Fortunately, the real culprit was discovered, and an innocent man's life was spared. Because of this near miscarriage of justice, the legislators and the Governor of New York acted with remarkable dispatch and celerity.

As of 1968, over seventy nations and thirteen states had abolished capital punishment. Israel permits capital punishment for but one cause: Nazi war crimes. To my knowledge, only Adolph Eichmann has gone to the gallows in the fledgling State. The Soviet Union, on the other hand, has reverted to medieval barbarism and has reinstituted execution for crimes against property. In the past few years, over 300 persons have been put to death for alleged "economic crimes"—half of whom were Jewish! In defending this primitive view of jurisprudence, Roman A. Rudenko, General Prosecutor of the Soviet Union, declared in *Izvestia* that "it is perfectly obvious that the measures for punishment provided for by Soviet law until now are insufficient for especially dangerous criminals, for such large-scale embezzlers of state property."

To be sure, we have come a long way since the days when in England, around 1800, there were 230 capital crimes, and a thirteen-year-old boy was hanged for stealing a spoon. We have reduced that number in most American states to 2 or 3 capital offenses. Moreover, we use the latest and most humane methods of slaughter.

The gas chamber and the electric chair are the modern refinements of the age-old practice of legal murder. In former times, criminals were executed by decapitation, hanging, boiling, burning, strangulation, stoning, etc. Today, we moderns have devised far more humane, far less brutal methods of execution by using cyanide gas or electric chairs. But the results are just as final, just as irrevocable.

Why?

What value does capital punishment possess?

What purpose does it serve?

Capital punishment has been defended on several grounds —all of which were advanced by the Bible in explaining the need for such penalties. First, it is maintained that a murderer must expiate his crime and atone for his sin by forfeiting his life. Second, it is argued that retribution must be meted out to the criminal—especially the murderer. "An eye for an eye" is the rule we must invoke when dealing with killers. Third—and this is the crux of the debate—the death penalty is defended as the greatest deterrent to extreme crimes such as murder or rape. The word "deterrent" means literally to "discourage by fear." The theory is that we discourage a potential murderer by the threat of the supreme penalty. We can dismiss the first two arguments as obsolete theology and can concentrate on the deterrent theory, for here, I think, the entire case stands or falls.

It is rather certain that the death penalty is *not* a deterrent to murder for several reasons. Murder is basically a crime of passion and a spontaneous act. The New York Police Department studied the 483 homocides committed in 1961 and found that most were not planned, were not connected with underworld activities, but were spontaneous acts. In fact, 206 of the homicides were the results of domestic disputes and occurred in the home! National studies confirm these data. About 80 to 90 per cent of murders are perpetrated in moments of jealous rage, blind passion, or drunken stupors. Surely the enraged husband who catches his wife *flagrante delicto* does not stop to ponder the dire consequences of his act before he dispatches her lover? Nor does the drunken thug reflect on the electric chair as he stabs his neighbor in a barroom brawl!

Furthermore, capital punishment does not deter the mentally ill, the psychotics, and the psychopaths, for whom the reality of a noose or a cyanide pellet holds no terrors. Many criminals fit into this category of the mentally disturbed.

The perfect crime is not prevented by the threat of execution either, for although the perfect criminal is fully aware of the consequences of his act, he never expects to get caught. The so-called professional killer is also not deterred by the threat of death. Criminologists have found that murder is a crime of the amateur and not the professional. Most professionals are too smart to sully their hands in such sanguinary business.

In point of fact, the deterrent theory is baseless. Pickpockets were hanged in the England of Charles Dickens, but at their hangings, other pickpockets had a field day in robbing the thousands who gathered to watch the executions. Most of the condemned criminals in English jails had in fact witnessed one or more hangings, with no apparent effect on their actions. On June 21, 1877, ten men were hanged in Pennsylvania for criminal conspiracy. The correspondent for the *New York Herald* wrote with enviable omniscience: "We may be certain that the pitiless severity of the law will deter the most wicked from anything like imitation of these crimes." Within the next two weeks, two witnesses and five prosecutors were murdered by the surviving members of the gang!

Statistics indicate, in fact, that states and nations without the death penalty have a lower murder rate than those with the supreme punishment. From 1931-40, the rate of murders in the United States was 8.1 per 100,000. In states without the death penalty the rate was 2.3 per 100,000. The seventy countries that have abolished capital punishment (including Israel) have the lowest murder rates in the world. Preliminary studies of New York State indicate no upward surge of homicides since the abolition of the death penalty. The deterrent theory—the pillar upon which those who advocate capital punishment build their structure—simply does not have any firm basis in fact.

But suppose we examine the Jewish position on the matter of capital punishment.

Even a casual reading of the Bible (especially the Pentateuch) gives one the impression that we Hebrews were a very sanguinary people. Beginning with the earliest passages in Genesis, we are told: "He who sheds the blood of a man shall have his blood shed in return; for in the image of God has He made man." [1] There are no less than thirty-seven crimes for which the death penalty is prescribed. Two stonings were actually carried out in the days of Moses. One was the execution of a blasphemer,[2] the other was the punishment of a Sabbath desecrator.[3]

Four standard methods of execution are described in grisly fashion in the second half of tractate Sanhedrin. Our sages ordered death by burning, stoning, strangulation, or decapitation for all manner of crimes ranging from murder to incest to cursing one's parents; yet, there was a vast gap between theory and practice already evident in Mishnaic times, some twenty centuries ago. In fact, the Mishnaic sages themselves admitted the abolition of the death penalty for the rebellious son, the suspected adulteress, the idolatrous city, etc.

All kinds of legal fictions were devised to render an execution almost impossible. For one thing, a court of twenty-three judges was required. Such a court could only adjudicate when the altar of the Temple was in use and the High Priest was officiating. The destruction of the Temple by the Romans in the year 70 C.E. ended any possibility of trying such cases. Furthermore, an entire group of penalties was removed from the jurisdiction of the "terrestrial court" and was remanded to the jurisdiction of the "celestial court."

The laws of testimony and evidence were so complicated and so severe (often reduced *ad absurdum*) as to make it almost impossible to convict a murderer. For example, relatives could not testify in court. Circumstantial evidence was inadmissible. Once Rabbi Judah ben Tabbai (first century B.C.E.) entered a ruin and found a slain man still writhing, and a sword still dripping blood was in the hand of the apparent slayer. Rabbi Judah was powerless to execute the culprit because circumstantial evidence was not sufficient for a conviction.[4]

Moreover, there had to be two eye-witnesses to the act, and they had to warn the potential killer of the enormity of his crime. He, in turn, had to declare in a defiant manner that irrespective of the consequences he was going to murder his victim! In addition, an accused could not incriminate himself or testify against himself. Where two eye-witnesses were lacking, the Beth Din could sentence the criminal to life imprisonment—but not death.[5] Obviously, no conviction could be obtained with such legal shackles.

The examination of witnesses by the judges was extremely thorough. The slightest contradiction in testimony —in facts, dates, events, or identities—invalidated the evidence. The judges impressed upon the witnesses the seriousness of their function and the graveness of the proceedings. Thus we read in Mishnah Sanhedrin:

How do the judges examine the witnesses in capital cases? They would bring them to their chambers and impress them with their awesome task. They would ask them: "Perhaps you are guessing? Perhaps you are heeding a rumor? Perhaps the evidence is hearsay? . . . Beware lest you make any mistake. For capital cases are not like civil cases . . . Human life is in your hands; and the blood of succeeding generations as well . . . Remember that man descended from one single ancestor to teach that whoever takes a single human life it is as if he had destroyed an entire world; while whoever saves a single life it is as if he had saved an entire world." [6]

If the court voted for acquittal by a majority of one, the accused went free. But a majority of two was needed to obtain a conviction. A judge could always change his mind for acquittal, but he could never reverse himself in favor of conviction. Double jeopardy was not permitted either.[7] In summing up the rabbinic attitude toward capital punishment, the Mishnah tells us:

If a Sanhedrin sentenced a person to death once in seven years it was considered a bloody court. Rabbi Eliezar ben Azariah said: "Once in seventy years." Rabbi Tarfon and Rabbi Akivah declared: "Were we sitting in the court, no one would ever be executed." [8]

On the rare occasions when an execution was carried out in early rabbinic times, every effort was made to mitigate the suffering as much as possible. The women of Jerusalem would offer the condemned a drugged wine to render him senseless.[9] Underlying this procedure was the Pharisaic teaching that one must choose as painless a death as possible for the condemned, for he too is a child of God. Likewise, he must be immediately lowered from the gibbet lest his dignity as a human being be impaired. And over each executed prisoner, Rabbi Meir informs us, the Divine Presence weeps and wails, for God regrets the death even of a wicked person.[10]

In medieval times, capital punishment was occasionally carried out in Spain. The Jewish Community was terrified over the existence of an informer or traitor (*moser*) in its midst, for the very future of the community hinged upon the testimony of such blackguards and unscrupulous scoundrels who, for a price, were prepared to betray their brethren without cause. Consequently, Jewish courts occasionally condemned such traitors to death, the sentence being carried out by the secular authorities. But, as Professor Yitzhak Baer has demonstrated in his masterly study of the Jews in Christian Spain, this was a case of Spanish Jewry borrowing from the Inquisition and the secular authorities a grisly and often illegal procedure that was at variance with Jewish law.

De facto, then, capital punishment was practically extinct in Jewish life even though *de jure* it remained on the books.

We have seen that capital punishment serves no constructive purpose and that it does not deter potential killers. But aside from this failure to eradicate the ills of the world, it exerts a pernicious effect on society. In the words of the medieval Tosafists: "It is a bad thing for everybody." [11] It cheapens human life and brutalizes humanity; it generates an atmosphere of public glee and sensationalism in the daily press and on radio and television in the best tradition of the Roman circus of old. As Clarence Darrow said well in defending Leopold and Loeb:

You may stand them up on the trap door of the scaffold and choke them to death, but that act will be infinitely more cold-blooded, whether justified or not, than any act that these boys have committed or can commit.

The state cannot preach reverence for life if it indulges in periodic judicial murders.

Capital punishment, moreover, takes its greatest toll from among the uneducated, the poor, and the deprived. Over half of the criminals executed in the United States since 1930 have been Negroes. Obviously, poor members of minority groups cannot engage the skilled lawyers needed to defend them against murder charges.

In addition, criminals are for the most part sick people who are in desperate need of psychiatrists and psychotherapy. Murderers act in their antisocial fashion because of a tangle of dark and sinister inner compulsions and drives beyond their control, which force them to commit brutal acts. In a remarkable letter published some time ago in the daily press, Dr. Anatole Holt, whose little daughter had been brutally murdered by a teen-age sex fiend, wrote the following eloquent appreciation of human frailty:

Had I caught the boy in the act, I would have wished to kill him. Now that there is no undoing of what is

> *done, I only wish to help him. Let no feeling of caveman-vengeance influence us. Let us, rather, help him who did so human a thing.*

We must, consequently, revise our concepts of punishment and revamp our theories of imprisonment. We must think in terms of rehabilitation, rather than revenge; of curing, rather than killing, of penitence, rather than punishment. That is what Ezekiel meant when he taught that "God does not desire the death of the sinner; rather that he repent and live." [12] A superb story in the Talmud [13] underscores the need for a compassionate theology and an enlightened approach to penology. Once, Beruria, the brilliant and scholarly wife of Rabbi Meir, overheard her husband praying for the death of a group of sinners who lived in the neighborhood. Rabbi Meir quoted Psalm 104:35 in his devotions: "Let sinners cease out of the earth and the wicked be no more." Beruria chastised him: "Do not pray for the death of *sinners*, my husband. Pray rather that *sins* cease out of the earth. Pray that the sinners may repent!" Meir did so—and the sinners repented.

Finally, there is always the possibility of error in executing an innocent man. Maine abolished capital punishment because an innocent man was hanged. Many people still maintain that Sacco and Vanzetti were blameless and never should have been executed. But no amount of remorse or regret can bring the executed victims back to life. As Benjamin Franklin wrote: "Better a hundred guilty people should escape, than one innocent man should suffer."

Every important church body—except the Catholic—has gone on record as opposing capital punishment. The leading Rabbinical groups—the Rabbinical Assembly, the

Central Conference of American Rabbis, the New York Board of Rabbis—have advocated the abolition of the death penalty. Each ghoulish episode, each legal murder, each near mistake gnaws at the consciences of decent men. How long the stench of seared flesh in the electrocution chamber? How long the pungent fumes of poison gas? How long the snapped and contorted necks? How long until man learns that "the judgement is God's" and not man's?

Only time will tell.

NOTES

1 Genesis 9:6
2 Leviticus 24:13-23
3 Numbers 15:32-36
4 Mekilta III, 170f; cf. Sanhedrin 37b
5 M. Sanhedrin IX, 5
6 M. Sanhedrin IV, 5
7 Mekilta III, 171f.
8 Makkot I, 10
9 Sanhedrin 43a; cf. Mark 15:23; Matthew 27:34
10 M. Sanhedrin VI, 5
11 Sanhedrin 3b, *s.v. moké lah*
12 Ezekiel 18:23
13 Berakhot 10a

VII

Civil Disobedience

"I say: Keep the king's command. . . ."
KOHELETH 8:2

OUR troubled times have encouraged troubling phenomena. None, perhaps, is more discordant and disturbing than the contempt for law and order that seems to be the order of the day—every day.

Ironically, the law-breakers are *not* merely gangsters and thugs; law-abiding citizens are involved. College students and civic leaders defy the draft in protest over what is (in their view) an immoral war. City workers in a great metropolis go on strike in violation of state law. All over the nation Civil Rights workers break local ordinances and municipal statutes. Southern governors and peace officers flout federal statutes and judicial decisions.

Why do people break the law? Why do so-called "decent" citizens and public officials, sworn to uphold the law, seek to destroy it?

One reason is that the *majority* may choose by *legal* means to destroy human rights. This happened in Nazi Germany; it happens in most dictatorships. In such cases, the only way to protest is by illegal means. Even in democratic nations it becomes essential to challenge the law and test the statutes.

Not all laws, for example, are just. Segregation laws were perfectly legal until quite recently. But if one believes that an unjust law is *no* law, then the citizen—such as the Civil Rights worker—has no alternative but to break it. This is especially true when the government is in league with evil. We are all too familiar with the double standard of justice that prevails in Mississippi and Alabama, where whites can lynch Negroes with impunity, and where police officials behave like stormtroopers.

Moreover, the judicial process of change is slow, sometimes too dilatory. Patience wears thin, and change may come too late. The wheels of justice frequently grind laboriously and ponderously, crushing human bodies and souls in the process. Dramatic demonstrations are often needed to focus attention and capture interest. Had the sit-in movement not aroused so much national interest in the plight of the Negro in America, the walls of inequity would still be unbreached.

Finally, it is sometimes necessary to break a law in order to test its legality. Many laws have been submitted to the courts for judicial review as a result of test-case arrests. Ironically, breaking the law may preserve democracy even as observing the law may undermine freedom.

The fundamental questions that have long perplexed man still remain, however. They are simply these: When is it proper to violate statutes and oppose the state? What criteria determine the legitimacy of civil disobedience? Was it proper for Americans to defy the Tax Act and the Stamp Act? Were they justified in frustrating Prohibition?

Was the Hagganah acting immorally in circumventing the White Paper? Do Southerners have the right to violate the Civil Rights Act? Are Civil Rights workers criminals for breaking municipal statutes? May violent techniques be employed?

The answers to these questions have been debated for centuries. Socrates studied the problem in ancient Athens. Plato writes in his *Crito*, man may *never* oppose the will of the state, for even if the law is wrong, the *greater* wrong is done by violating the law. In our own country, Henry David Thoreau came to a very different conclusion. In his essay "Civil Disobedience" he wrote: "I think that we should be men first and subjects afterward. It is not desirable to cultivate a respect for the law, so much as for the right." The Greeks and Romans, then, viewed the state as all powerful, and the monarch as absolute. This philosophy can, as we in our own time have learned, destroy man and crush freedom. The humanist of the Thoreau stripe, on the other hand, would rely on subjective canons of morality and the dictates of conscience. Without an absolute standard of morality, however, society can end in anarchy. And if we are to rely on conscience alone, who knows what bizarre results may emerge? As Samuel Butler put it: "Conscience is thoroughly well-bred and soon leaves off talking to those who do not wish to hear it."

And therein lies the dilemma of civil disobedience.

What says Judaism on this controversial matter? Is the state all powerful? Does the monarch enjoy divine rights? Dare men break the law?

At first blush it would appear that the Jewish civilization was no different from other ancient empires or medieval monarchies. The king was supreme—"the annointed of the

Lord." Wisdom Literature is particularly conservative, reflecting (in the judgment of Robert Gordis) the upperclass morality of the ancient Middle East. Thus the Proverbs counsel "not to get involved with those who seek change," [1] for "by the will of the Lord does the monarch reign." [2] Koheleth declares: "I say: Keep the king's command. . . . Since the king's word is law, who can say to him, 'What are you doing?' " [3] The Talmud sets down the rule that "one who rebels against the monarch is to be executed." [4]

But this is not the whole story. Judaism harbored a revulsion toward the absolute monarch from its earliest days. The Book of Deuteronomy laid down restrictions on his power and wealth: "Be sure to set a king over yourself one of your own people. . . . Moreover, he shall not keep many horses, or send people back to Egypt to add to his horses. . . . And he shall not have many wives, lest his heart go astray; nor shall he amass silver and gold to excess. When he is seated on his royal throne, he shall have a copy of this Torah . . . let him read in it all his life, so that he may learn to revere the Lord his God, to observe faithfully every word of this Torah as well as these laws. Thus he will not act haughtily towards his fellows or deviate from the Torah to the right or to the left. . . ." [5] In the Proverbs and Psalms the ruler is cautioned to conduct his affairs in truth, justice, and mercy.

The prophet Samuel had warned against the monarchy even before Saul was proclaimed King of Israel. He predicted that Israel's kings would be no different from their pagan counterparts. "The King will take your sons into the army . . . and your daughters will become his slaves and domestics; your best fields and vineyards and olive or-

chards will be given to his eunuchs and slaves. . . . He
will take a tithe of your sheep and you will be his slaves." [6]
It was Samuel's view that only *one* King could reign over
Israel, and that was the Lord Himself. The sages who discuss the passage are divided as to its meaning. Some believe
that the Prophet was enunciating the absolute right of
kings; others maintain that he was alerting the people to
the dangers inherent in the kingship.[7] The plain meaning
of the passage supports the latter view.

Contempt for the monarchy reached its apogee in the
days of the iniquitous kings of Israel and Judah. As Hosea
bitterly wails: "Ho, now, your king, that he may save you
in all your cities! And your judges, of whom you said,
'Give me a king and princes!' I give you a king in Mine
anger, and take him away in My wrath." [8] This contempt
was further heightened during the corrupt reigns of the
Hasmoneans and Herod, whose ruthless tyranny turned
the hearts of the people against them.

Obviously, Biblical Judaism did not adopt the popular
Middle-Eastern view that the monarch was an omnipotent
demigod who enjoyed the power of life and death over his
subjects. God alone was king—the monarch was merely
the political-military leader of the people, answerable to
them and bound by God's Torah.

Rabbinic Judaism accepted the opinion of the great third-
century Babylonian scholar, Mar Samuel, that "the law of
the kingdom is law" [9]—an opinion "more frequently invoked than clarified," to quote Professor Salo W. Baron.
This famous principle seems to give absolute rights to the
monarch and apparently denies the right of civil disobedience.

Yet the sages of ancient and medieval Judaism limited its

application so as to curtail despotism. They deliberately avoided a maximal interpretation.

Naturally the principle of "the law of the kingdom is law" was not a license for the destruction of human life. The normative Jewish view on the question was crystallized in the days of the Roman Emperor Hadrian in the second century C.E. The scholars held that one may comply with all the ruler's decrees, even if one thereby violates Jewish law, except three: One may never commit idolatry, sexual immorality, or murder, even if ordered to do so at sword's point.[10] The Talmud puts it this way: "If the governor orders you to kill or be killed, you must submit to martyrdom rather than murder another human being. For who says that your blood is any redder than his?" Since humiliation is likened to murder,[11] we can presume that we are duty bound to resist shaming other humans even if the law requires us to do so.

The monarch may not destroy the principles of the Jewish religion, nor is any Jew required to remain loyal to his king if that king is intent on uprooting the faith or precepts of the Torah. Talmudic law ruled that a Jew must not publicly comply with even the slightest variation in Jewish practice if the monarch's intention in ordering such procedures was the destruction of the Jewish faith. If, on the other hand, the monarch's intention was not insidious, and he was merely seeking to gratify his personal whims, then one might acquiesce in his orders even if it entailed a violation of all but the three cardinal principles.[12] "Do not oppose the laws of the state—even unjust ones—unless they are designed to uproot the Sabbath, the *mitzvot*, or the Torah," said the sages.[13] "If a [Jewish or pagan] king issues a decree to annul a single *mitzvah* we do not heed him," opined Maimonides.[14] Maimonides—doubtlessly influenced by his troubled youth when his family pretended to be Moslems in order to survive the fanatical Almohade reign in Spain—admonished his readers to flee such a despotic country at the first opportunity, or else be guilty of apostasy.

The Jewish monarch was limited in his arbitrariness. He was considered the annointed of the Lord—never a deity himself. His *authority* was divine in origin—not his *person*. If he transgressed the *mitzvot* he was to be treated like any ordinary layman.[15] Likewise, the sages taught that the verse, "You shall not curse a prince of your people" [16] applies only when the prince conducts himself according to the practices of the Jewish people.[17]

The Talmudic rabbis also curbed the judicial powers of the monarch. They did so not because the king was above the law, but because they had been intimidated by Alexander Jannaeus and Herod, whose appearances before the Sanhedrin had been a mockery of justice.[18] As a result, they decided that the monarch would no longer be permitted to judge or be judged. And they did more: they ruled that he could initiate a war only with the permission of the Great Sanhedrin of 71 judges.[19]

Medieval scholars went farther in restricting the application of Mar Samuel's dictum. They applied the principle to gentile, not Jewish sovereigns. In a remarkable passage, Rabbi Nissim Gerondi of Spain (fourteenth century) wrote that "the rule of 'the law of the kingdom is law' applies only to a gentile king, for the land is his and he may threaten the Jews with expulsion if they fail to keep his commandments; but not to Jewish kings, since all of Israel are partners in the land of Israel." Moreover, the principle was applicable in the realm of civil, not religious law. Secular law, ruled the rabbis, must prevail in payment of taxes and customs, the use of legal tender, contracts and notes, and the king's right of eminent domain. In all other areas, Jewish legal norms were to govern Jewish life.

There were limitations set to the power of secular law, however. Rabbi Jacob Tam, who lived in the Rhineland in the days of the Second Crusade, declared that the monarch's laws are supreme "when he applies his laws equally to all inhabitants of the realm; but when he varies from state to state the rule does not apply." The famous German scholar, Rabbi Meir of Rothenberg (thirteenth century), stated several times in his responsa that the monarch who imposes new and unprecedented taxes that discriminate against groups or individuals is not to be obeyed. "This is not the 'law of the kingdom' but the 'lawlessness of the kingdom,' " he wrote. Maimonides sums up the general consensus of medieval schools in his *Code* [20] where he records that illegal usurpations, arbitrary levies, and prejudicial laws that discriminate against one class or craft or segment of the population are illegal and immoral. A king who ordains such decrees is considered a robber (*gazlan*), and his laws are invalid.

In sum: the monarch is *not* all powerful, and the state is *not* necessarily supreme. Man does have the right to oppose the laws of the land under certain circumstances.

Do we have examples of civil disobedience in Jewish history? Indeed we have. Ancient Egypt produced classic illustrations of disobedience to tyrannical Pharaohs. When the two heroic midwives refused to kill the Hebrew male infants at birth in violation of Pharaoh's instructions [21] they were being disobedient to the king. An extraordinary legend (no doubt reflective of Roman, rather than Egyptian times) informs us that the Jewish police in Egypt suffered severely rather than betray and mistreat their fellow Jews who were enslaved to Pharaoh. They were violating the "law of the kingdom" because of a higher law of God.[22] The rebellion of Moses against Pharaoh represents the ultimate in civil disobedience, for here we have a man who led a horde of slaves who refused to remain docile subjects of a tyrant and chose to fight for freedom and dignity.

What better illustrations have we of civil disobedience in action than the lives of the Prophets? Nathan dramatized the concept when he pointed an accusing finger at David, condemning him for adultery and murder.[23] Elijah was disobedient when he took King Ahab to task for stealing Nabot's vineyard after having sent him unjustly to his execution.[24] Nor should we forget the examples of Isaiah and Amos and Jeremiah who courted death rather than knuckle to inequity and despotism.

The Maccabean Revolt is another illustration of civil disobedience. Rather than accept forced Hellenization and the spiritual genocide of Judaism, the Maccabees led the Jews of Palestine in a bloody war against King Antiochus and his laws. And when Hannah and her seven sons sacrificed their lives rather than conform to the monarch's decrees to bow to idols, they carried on in the same spirit.

The Bar Kokhba revolt was similarly motivated. Emperor Hadrian had proscribed the study of Torah, the practice of circumcision, and the full observance of Judaism, on penalty of death. All was perfectly legal (the Romans were, after all, masters of the law), and there were those who exhorted the sages and populace to comply with the law. Yet, faced with the certain obliteration of Judaism, Bar Kokhba (evidently encouraged by the martyr Rabbi Akivah) rose up in rebellion. The rebels were committed to the idea that the Lord above was king—not Hadrian or any other flesh-and-blood ruler. The teachers of Torah willingly paid with their lives rather than acquiesce in the dissolution of the Jewish religion. Rabbi Akivah persistently taught Torah in jail, even with his last breath.

The Warsaw Ghetto uprising is another case in point. A weak, half-starved, poorly-armed band of desperate Jews rose up against their Nazi exterminators in a doomed attempt to die with honor rather than march like sheep to the slaughter. And the *Yishuv's* struggle with the British in Palestine prior to 1948 must be judged in the same light as the struggle of an oppressed People for freedom and justice —tyrannical law notwithstanding. Had the Jewish community abided by British law and not armed and trained for conflict, the Arabs would doubtlessly have made good on their promise to "push the Zionists into the Sea."

There are, of course, less dramatic, less sanguinary illustrations of civil disobedience in Jewish life. The right to strike is one such illustration. Talmudic law explicitly guarantees that right when it rules: "A worker may withdraw from work even in the middle of the day." [25] True, the worker may not do so if he thereby causes unreasonable damage; [26] nor may he strike merely to blackmail the employer into paying higher wages. He may, however, resort to this strategy in order to assert his freedom, or to improve improper or unhealthy working conditions.

In our long history, we Jews have been a loyal, law-abiding nation, but when our faith was endangered, and our moral principles challenged, we resisted and fought. It was unthinkable for the Prophets or Pharisees to argue that the state can do no wrong; that the government is omnipotent; that the king is above the law. Hemlock was for Socrates, not Jeremiah.

Yes, Judaism preached that man must be law-abiding; that a society of laws is his best hope. "Pray for the welfare of the government. For without the government, man would swallow his neighbor alive." [27] Rabbi Janai warned that the fear of the government must always hang over man,[28] but one can be perfectly law-abiding, and at the same time, bestial beyond words. The Nazi war criminals all argued that they were not guilty of genocide for they were merely following orders. And so they were. From 1933 to 1945, it was the law of the land in Germany to annihilate Jews. Citizens who violated that law were criminals. Consequently, Adolph Eichmann was technically a law-abiding citizen, while Pastor Heinrich Grüber, who hid Jews from their pursuers, was a criminal and enemy of the state. Obviously, civil disobedience is proper in certain instances, and violent opposition is valid when life is at stake and freedom in jeopardy.

What emerges from the Jewish understanding of civil disobedience is this: Man must consider whether transcendent values are at stake when he resorts to civil disobedience; he must weigh the means resorted to in his disobedience so that they are commensurate with the values at stake; he must scrutinize Jewish tradition to determine whether civil disobedience is sanctioned failing legal means of redressing grievances.

When human life is endangered, then all means may be utilized—yes, even bloodshed—if no alternative presents itself. "If one comes to kill you," rules the Talmud, "you may preemptively kill him in self defense." [29] When human freedom and dignity are jeopardized, then man may turn to strikes and boycotts, tax evasions, and stratagems. When man's religious and moral principles are at stake, then he has every right to protest, to rally, to petition, to resort to subterfuge and illegal acts to defend those principles. Soviet Jews who study Torah and practice Judaism clandestinely are violating man's law. But they are defending a Higher Law. They may be criminals in the eyes of a brutal State; they are martyrs in the view of Heaven.

The danger to this approach is that quixotic conscience may prompt civil disobedience and give birth to anarchy, lawlessness, and chaos. In the name of Civil Rights, cities have been burned, and innocent people killed. That is why the religious Jew believes that conscience cannot be trusted alone; it must be constantly shaped and sharpened, hammered and honed by Jewish law and ethics, traditions, and values. Man's ultimate criterion must be found in the Book —in the word of God and the hallowed traditions of humanity. For there is a higher law than man's—God's law. That law must mold our consciences and dictate when we must risk all, even our lives, against the mightiest forces of the state. "To sin by silence when they should protest," said Abraham Lincoln, "makes cowards out of men." Silence is not always golden. There are moments in life when obedience to God summons man to rebellion against the forces that would destroy human freedom and degrade human dignity. That is a proper understanding of civil disobedience; in reality, it is a sacred obedience. And there is no higher obedience than that which moves man to give everything for God, sacrificing all for the sacred principles and eternal values of life, liberty, freedom, and human dignity.

NOTES

1 Proverbs 24:21
2 Proverbs 8:15
3 Koheleth 8:2,4
4 Sanhedrin 49a
5 Deuteronomy 17:14-20
6 I Samuel 8:11-18
7 Tosefta Sanhedrin IV, 3
8 Hosea 13:10,11
9 Baba Kama 113; Baba Batra 54bf; Gittin 10b; Nedarim 28a
10 Yoma 85b; Sanhedrin 74a; Pesahim 25b
11 Baba Metzia 58b
12 Sanhedrin 72af.
13 Tanhuma *Noah* pp. 196 ff.
14 Maimonides, *Code*, "Kings," III, 8,9; "Foundations of Torah," V, 1-4,
15 Tosefta Sanhedrin IV,2

16 Exodus 22:27
17 Mekilta III, 152
18 Josephus, *Antiquities*, XIV, 9,4; Sanhedrin 18a,b
19 Maimonides, *Code*, "Kings," V, 2
20 Maimonides, *Code*, "Kings," V, 13
21 Exodus 1:16-22
22 Numbers Rabbah XV, 20
23 IIS 12
24 IK 21
25 Baba Metziah 77a
26 *Shulhan Arukh, Hoshen Mishpat* § 333
27 Avot III, 2
28 Menahot 98a
29 Sanhedrin 72a; Berakhot 58b

VIII

The Religious Roots of
Anti-Semitism

"In return for my love they are my adversaries. . . ."
PSALMS 109:4

GAZING at the ordinary, average features of Adolph Eichmann, I kept asking myself: "What makes a seemingly normal human being a virulent, maniacal monster and ruthless butcher of Jews?" I had watched the Eichmann trial on television night after night; then I observed it in person in Jerusalem. And still the answer to my query eluded me. That Eichmann was no psychopath was certain: his fifteen years of normal living had proved the fact. What, then, was the core of his malevolent anti-Semitism? And what, in a larger sense, is the cause of anti-Semitism?

Many interpretations of this disease have been given. Each specialist advances his own diagnosis—the psychologist offers psychological reasons, the sociologist adduces sociological causes, and the economist cites economic factors.

I have reached the conclusion that these explanations are

merely ancillary to the truth. Since the days of Emperor Constantine's conversion to Christianity the religious factor has been the *primary* cause of Jew-hatred. The seeds had been implanted in the Gospels; the Church Fathers nurtured them; the Papacy cultivated the saplings; the spiritual lights and theologians of Catholicism and Protestantism raised them to full height; the masses of Christians harvested the bitter fruits.

The Dean of the Episcopal Cathedral of Saint Paul in Boston, the Very Reverend Charles H. Bucks, Jr., once declared in a sermon: "The basic document of anti-Semitism in the Western World is the New Testament. And until the church admits this, and teaches its people to distinguish between the gospel of Jesus and the anti-Semitism of some of the human authors of the New Testament books, this terrible problem will not begin to be solved."

How sad—but how true! The Gospels, edited and slanted by the Church Fathers, whose anti-Semitism was unbridled, reflect fierce prejudices against Jews—the Pharisees and hypocrites so often demeaned in the pages of the Christian Bible. The Fourth Gospel is especially virulent; it is John who absolves Pilate and the Romans and indicts the Jews for the alleged crucifixion of Jesus. What more bloodthirsty canard has appeared in world literature than Matthew 27:25: "His blood be upon us and our children forever." How that phrase has struck responsive chords in Christian hearts! And how it has sent a shudder of terror in Jewish souls!

The fact that reputable scholars like Solomon Zeitlin among Jews, and James Parkes among Christians, have cast serious doubts on the veracity of the Gospel account of the

Crucifixion has mattered little. The fact that three Gospels lay the onus on the Romans and realize that Jesus himself longed for death as part of the Divine Plan has been overlooked. The fact that deicide is a theological absurdity (for who can kill God?) has been shunted aside. "Forgive them Father, they know not what they do" [1] has been replaced by the bloodcurdling imprecation of Matthew.

The Church Fathers shaped the Christian faith in much the same fashion as the Talmudic rabbis formulated Judaism. And it was due to the writings of the Church Fathers that Judeo-Christian relations were poisoned and embittered. In the words of James Parkes: "The true explanation of anti-Semitism is to be found in the history of the early centuries of Christianity, the daughter-religion of Judaism, in the theology evolved by the Church, in the interpretation of the Old Testament that became current among her theologians and preachers, and in the legislation which was inspired by these interpretations."

Let us survey briefly the writings, commentaries, and preachings of those founders of the church.

Tertullian (d. 222) read in the Cain-Abel tragedy an adumbration of Judeo-Christian relations. Cain, the elder brother (Judaism), slew Abel, the younger brother (Jesus). As a result, Cain was condemned to wander over the face of the earth with a brand of shame on his face. Still, he was not to be killed; God wanted him preserved as an eternal witness.

Justin Martyr in the second century, saw the destruction of the Temple and the dispersion of the Jewish people as fitting punishment for rejecting Jesus.

John Chrysostom, "The Golden Mouth" (d. 407), was one of the most vitriolic anti-Semites. The Syrian Jew-baiter delivered eight venomous sermons against the Jews. The Jews, he preached, were not in error when they crucified Jesus: "The Jews erred not ignorantly but with full knowledge." And he declared:

> *The Synagogue is worth no more than the theatre . . . it is a place of prostitution, it is a den of thieves and a hiding place of wild animals. . . . God has abandoned them [the Jews], what hope of salvation have they left? . . . Since they have disowned the Father, crucified the Son, and rejected the Spirit's help, who would not dare to assert that the synagogue is a home of demons! God is not worshiped there; it is simply a house of idolatry. . . . The Jews live for their bellies, they crave for the goods of this world. In shamelessness and greed they surpass even the pigs and goats. . . . You should turn away from them as from a pest and a plague of the human race.*

As if this were not enough, Chrysostom added: "I hate the synagogue. . . . I hate the Jews for the same reason;" not men, but "God has brought you misfortunes—for God hates you."

Constantine the Great, whose conversion to Christianity in 313 sealed the fate of Judaism, spoke of the synagogue as a *conciliabulum* (brothel).

Jerome, in the fifth century, described the Jewish houses of worship as "the synagogue of Satan."

Augustine (d. 430), greatest of the early church theologians, wrote that the Jews slew Jesus, and were dispersed by God as punishment. The Jews, he declared, are the enemies of the church and blind to the truth. Consequently, they are condemned to perpetual servitude ". . . your brother shall you serve." [2] Still, wrote the Bishop of Hippo, the Jews ought not to be annihilated, because they are the possessors of the books of the Bible. Moreover, they must bear testimony to the truth of Scripture; their servitude will be witness to all the nations that the prophecies concerning Jesus the Christ were true.

Why were the Church Fathers so intent on poisoning Jewish-Christian relations? There are several reasons.

The Church felt constrained to cut the Gordian knot, to set a course apart from the mother-faith. Judeo-Christian relations were too close; the boundaries were fluid, and adherents of both faiths engaged in friendly intercourse with one another. Chrysostom clearly indicates this motive when he chides the Syrian Christians for attending the synagogue services on Rosh Hashanah and for keeping the Sabbath and other Jewish rites.

Moreover, the Church had to combat the pagan challenge as to why the Jews, the Chosen People themselves, refused to acknowledge Jesus. Hence, the Fathers of the Church discredited the Jews and their understanding of the Bible. The blind and obdurate Jews simply failed to see in Jesus the fruition of their Messianic hopes.

The technique to discredit Judaism was that of "the teaching of contempt" and the "system of degradation"— to borrow Jules Isaac's apt phrases. Jews were depicted as degenerates—ossified relics of a former glorious faith. Their laws and rituals were reviled and condemned. They were branded "sensualists," while Christians were the "spiritual" people. They were called a blind and refractory people who misunderstood and rejected Jesus.

God, through his Prophets, had denounced and reproved

Israel, taught the Fathers. The curses of the Hebrew Bible against the Jews were externalized and seen as eternal damnation by God for the People who failed to perceive the truth of Christianity.

Jews were described as "deicides"—people who had murdered God's son. Their punishment was the destruction of their Temple and their perpetual statelessness and wandering. They, and not the Romans, were indicted for the crucifixion. Indeed, the Coptic Orthodox Church made Pontius Pilate a saint!

Although formerly the Chosen People, the Jews were now rejected by God. The New Israel was the Church; the New Testament had superceded the Old. The synagogue of the Jews was the synagogue of Satan; they were a devilish people, in league with demonic forces.

The Jewish roots of Christianity were denied; Jesus and the disciples were depicted as Christians, not Jews. The Marcionite heresy even went so far as to urge the expunging of the Hebrew Bible from the Christian canon. Although the Marcionites were excommunicated in 144, their attitude, remarks Professor Abraham Joshua Heschel, has prevailed in Catholic and Protestant thinking to our day.

All of these Patristic teachings against Judaism encrusted the Christian mentality "even to the depths of its subconscious," wrote Jules Isaac, and shaped the myth and caricature of the Jew.

That the Church Fathers were successful in their campaign is evident from the development of Christian-Roman law and subsequent Canon law, as well as medieval Church thinking. The great law codes of Justinian and Theodotian codified Patristic anti-Semitism. The law forbade the construction of new synagogues and condoned plundering of such edifices. It considered conversion to Judaism a capital crime of treason, and ordered Jews to "restrain their rites" and lower the sound of their liturgy lest they offend their Christian neighbors. It forbade Jews to hold Christian slaves, and proscribed them from holding public office or serving in the military, for the slave must never hold dominion over the master.

The law sought to interfere with Jewish worship by insisting that the Scriptures be read in Greek, rather than Hebrew. It proscribed the study of the Oral Law of the Mishnah and Talmud as an erroneous contrivance of men.

In these laws of the fourth and fifth centuries lie the sources of medieval Canon law concerning the Jews. The entire structure of medieval thinking vis-à-vis Judaism and the nature of the Papacy's dealings with its detested mother-faith were rooted in the early centuries of the Church's development.

The rôle of the Papacy in Judeo-Christian relations was ambivalent and complex. It represented a medley of love and hate, of toleration and contempt, of concern and condemnation. As Professor Solo W. Baron writes in his masterly and judicious analysis of the problem,[3] the Papacy followed a traditional policy of general sufferance with severe qualifications. Its attitude was fairly constant, and the Jews often turned to the Holy See for protection since a perpetual dichotomy existed between the Papacy and the local and provincial leaders of the Church. Ironically, Jews would not have survived without the intervention of Rome.

What was the policy of the Papacy toward the Jewish people? The Papacy was committed to the idea that Jews must be preserved, albeit in a degraded and subservient state. Gregory the Great set this theme in his famous Bull,[4] *circa* 600:

> *Therefore, just as the Jews in their synagogues must not have the license to undertake anything beyond what the law permits them, so ought they not suffer, contrary to justice and an equitable order, any prejudice and diminution in their rights.*

Why? Because Scripture warned the Christians not to destroy them, and Jesus Himself prayed for them. They must be preserved as testimony to the truth of the Christian faith. They were not heathens or idolators—they were still the guardians of the truth of the Old Testament, Israel in the flesh, if not in the spirit. Ultimately, wrote Thomas Aquinas, they would be converted and would usher in the second coming of Christ. Until then, Christians must tolerate their privately held blasphemies "out of mildness of christian piety," which was Pope Alexander III's phrase and "from pure grace and pity," as Pope Clement II put it.

There was even a practical reason for the Papacy's toleration of the Jews—money. Jews assured the Holy See a steady flow of gold and silver in tax monies for the ever-impoverished coffers of the popes. This fact accounts for the relative stability of Jews in the Papal States throughout the Middle Ages. Thus, while Jews were being expelled from such places as England, France, Spain, Portugal, the Italian duchies, and the German city-states, they found a haven in Rome, Avignon, Ancona, and Carpentras, among other places. Since they were not bound by the rules of

Canon Law that considered usury a mortal sin, they served the vital (albeit execrable) function of usurers and pawn brokers in the Christian society: "It is better that this people should perpetrate usury than that Christians should engage in it with one another," declared Pope Nicholas V.

Beginning with Calixtus II (1119-24), a *Constitutio pro Judaeis* was regularly issued (really to Roman Jewry) based on Gregory's *Sicut Judaeis*. These Papal constitutions for the Jews warned them not to arrogate to themselves new laws, but Christians were similarly enjoined not to wound or kill the Jews or take their money without authority. Nor might they baptize Jews forcibly or desecrate their cemeteries or prevent them from keeping their festivals. Violators were threatened with bans of excommunication.

There was, however, a dangerous loophole in the constitution, a loophole that was destined to vitiate the Papal protection in the ages to come, for the decree did not apply to Jews "plotting against the Christian religion." How that phrase became a pretext for all manner of persecutions!

With the Crusades, Papal protection diminished, and the *Constitutio pro Judaeis* remained a dead letter. While the Church did not inaugurate the anti-Jewish riots of the Crusades, it never effectively punished the criminals. Pope Urban II never condemned the murderers of the First Crusade; only John, Bishop of Spires, took forceful action. Pope Gregory IX and John XXII did admonish the ruffians and called for protection by the nobles and bishops, but there the matter ended: there was no excommunication, no outspoken denunciation, no condemnatory sermon or encyclical. From Urban II to Pius XII, the Church has remained silent where suffering Jews have been involved.

Pressures on the Jews to convert were constantly exerted by the Church. True forcible baptisms were discouraged and condemned. As Thomas Aquinas wrote (restating the views of Augustine, Gregory the Great, etc.), Jews should not be forced to the faith, "for belief is a matter of will."

This view, however, was open to widely divergent interpretations. Coercion by threat of expulsion was considered proper. And if conversion was coerced without *direct physical* violence, it was valid.

Thomas Aquinas disapproved of baptizing children without parental consent, but there were popes and theologians who demurred. Innocent III wrote in 1201 that *fait accompli* it was valid, since the baptism redeemed the children from original sin. Others argued that since the Jews were slaves of the prince (*servi camerae*), their children belonged to the prince. And more: God has a greater claim over the child than the parents because the soul is divine. There were those who even argued that a child over twelve had a mind of his own and could freely choose baptism. And acid-tongued Duns Scotus—the gentle soul who suggested that some "sample" Jews be kept alive forever on a distant island as witnesses to Christian truth—urged forcible conversion of children since God's rights preceded parental rights.

Officially, the view of Aquinas prevailed; in practice the malevolent view won out. Thus, in 1858, little Edgar Mortara was kidnapped from his parental home in Bologna on the pretext that his Christian nurse had secretly baptized him during a severe illness. World protests notwithstanding, Pope Pius IX remained obdurate, and the child was raised in the Holy Orders, never to rejoin his parents or his ancestral faith again.

Even in our day, in the wake of the tragedy of World War II, some 10,000 Jewish children sequestered by Christian benefactors in homes, nunneries, and monasteries, are being raised as Christians, and have never been reunited with kith or kin!

Apart from missionary pressures, the policy of degradation of the medieval Jew was clearly seen in the segregation program of the Church. Left to their own devices, Jews and Christians got along rather well; they lived near one another, they visited one another's homes, they even attended divine services in one another's house of worship. But this was scandalous to the Church leaders; social intercourse was to cease forever. Innocent III stated the case in a letter to the Count of Nevers in 1208:

The Lord made Cain a wanderer and a fugitive over the earth, but set a mark upon him, making his head to shake, lest any finding him should slay him. Thus the Jews, against whom the blood of Jesus Christ calls out, although they ought not be killed, lest the Christian people forget the Divine Law, yet as wanderers ought they to remain upon the earth, until their countenance be filled with shame and they seek the name of Jesus Christ, the Lord. That is why blasphemers of the Christian name ought not be aided by Christian princes to oppress the servants of the Lord, but ought rather be forced into the servitude of which they made themselves deserving when they raised

> *sacrilegious hands against Him Who had come to con-*
> *fer true liberty upon them, thus calling down His*
> *blood upon themselves and upon their children.*

The third Lateran Council, in 1179, had threatened to excommunicate Christians who presumed to live with Jews. Innocent III and his fourth Lateran Council in 1215 went further. Jews were to have no relations, either sexual or social, with Christians. They were not to employ Christian nurses and servants, and they were to wear a badge of shame that lumped them together with lepers, vagrants, and prostitutes—a rule that degraded them even more and marked them for contempt and mayhem. Later Councils, for example, at Basel, in 1434, forbade attendance at Jewish parties or weddings. The sixteenth century witnessed the culmination of the segregation of the Jews with the institution of the ghetto (originally, the word meant "iron foundry"—the site of the first Venetian ghetto)—an enclosed, fetid, lugubrious, and unsalutary quarter in which hundreds and even thousands of Jews were packed like sardines. The gates were locked at night, Jews could sally forth only with a permit to do business outside, houses could only be expanded upward (never outward on new lands), synagogues (as in the *cinque scuole* of Rome) were often piled on top of one another in one structure, like a layer cake. The segregation policy of the Church was eminently successful.

Not content with a policy of rigorous segregation, the Papacy sought to implement a brutal system of economic, political, and social discrimination. In 1081 Gregory VII admonished King Alphonso VI of Castille to "cease to suffer the Jews to rule over Christians and exercise authority over them, for to allow Jews to judge Christians "is the same as to oppress God's Church and to exalt the synagogue of Satan."

Jews were not to hold Christian servants, slaves, or nurses. They were not to practice medicine on Christian patients—although popes often consulted Jewish doctors. Their testimony was suspect because of their "perfidy" (*perfidia Judaeorum*), so they were subjected to a degrading form of oath (*more judaico*). They were excluded from most economic fields—land-owning, agriculture, real estate, guilds—and reduced to the odious tasks of usury and dealing in old clothes. They were not to work on Christian holidays, or to appear in public on Good Friday.

Worse yet: they were compelled by papal order to listen to conversionist sermons—often in their own synagogues and often at their own expense. As Pope Leo VII wrote to the Archbishop of Mayence in 937: "You should never cease preaching to them . . . the belief in the Sacred Trinity and the mystery of the Lord's incarnation. . . . Should they, however, refuse to believe, you shall expel them from your states with our permission. For we ought not associate with the Lord's enemies. . . ." Jews were even required to pay for the upkeep of the houses for converts—the *Domus conversorum* in London and the House of Catechumens in Rome.

The most degrading Papal Bull discriminating against Jews was the infamous *Cum nimis absurdum* of Pope Paul IV, issued on July 12, 1555, and described by Cecil Roth as "one of the landmarks in the history of human persecution and of Jewish martyrdom." Outraged by the "absurd" gall of the Roman Jews who dared to live in decent homes, wear fine clothes, and associate in dignity with Christian neighbors, the Pope ordered Jews into a ghetto. They were to wear a badge of shame, they were never to associate with Christians, they were restricted from most economic practices, they were to possess no more than one synagogue in each city, and so on. Hitler and Stalin improved but little on this Bull of the Prince of the Church.

One of the more humiliating touches adopted by the popes concerned the Roman Jewish community. At the coronation ceremony, Roman Jewry would greet the new pope in order to receive a renewal of his protection. The delegation would carry a scroll of the Torah, which they would extend to him. Each pope would bless the Jews generally and admonish them that while the Church revered the Torah, it deplored the fact that Jews remained blind to the truth of the Gospels. Some of the popes committed the ultimate indignity of dropping the Torah to the ground, to the mortification of the Jewish delegation.

This contempt for even the Hebrew Bible was symptomatic of the Papacy's contempt for Jewish literature, especially the Talmud. Spurred on by apostates, Franciscans, and Dominicans, Jewish literature was censored, mutilated, burned, and confiscated. Time after time, copies of the Talmud were burned. In Paris, for example, in 1240, forty carloads of the Talmud went up in flames. So thorough was the process that only one complete European manuscript of the Talmud written prior to the twelfth century is extant. And the number of volumes seized by popes and nobles is appalling! It is small wonder that the Vatican houses one of the largest Hebrew manuscript collections in the world.

We must not overlook papal anti-Semitism as expressed in prayers, homilies, and sermons. Pope Galasius, at the end of the fifth century, was the innovator of the Good Friday prayer, *pro perfidis Judaeis*, which ran like this: "We pray also for the unbelieving (*perfidis*) Jews that our God and Lord should remove the veil from their hearts, and they should themselves recognize our Lord Jesus Christ." Only with the advent of Pope John XXIII in our day has this prayer "for the perfidious Jews" been expunged.

As to sermons and homilies, the popes were especially fond of the parable of Cain and Abel as adumbrating the conflict of Church and Synagogue. Biblical texts were quoted and misquoted, distorted and contorted, to fit papal purposes. Thus Gregory the Great saw in the Jacob-Esau conflict a prophecy that the Jews (namely, Esau!) would serve the Christians (namely, Jacob).[5] Of course, Matthew 27:25 was a popular text to remind the listeners that the deicides themselves acknowledged their eternal guilt. And Genesis 21:10,[6] in which Abraham is told to cast out the bondmaid Hagar and her son Ishmael, is taken to mean "cast out the Jews" from Christian lands.

When all else failed, the popes resorted to forced disputations—unequal contests in which the Jewish sages were pitted against apostates and churchmen. In Paris in 1240, in Barcelona in 1263, and in Tortosa in 1413-14, these sorry spectacles attracted huge crowds of nobles and clerics. And each time, the pressures for conversion mounted: Perhaps 25,000 Jews converted after the Tortosa dispute.

In view of the foregoing evidence of papal ambivalence, is it any wonder that "papal protection," to quote Solomon Grayzel, "fell far short of even its limited goal?" True, without even this limited, half-hearted concern for the Jews by the Papacy, we would never have survived. But how much more could the pontiffs have done to ease the suffering of the Jews! How much more benevolence and protection could they have displayed! How different things might have been if only. . . .

We have noted that there was a dichotomy between the Papacy and local church officials. If the Holy See was intent on preserving the Jewish people and—in its feeble way —protected Jewish rights, local clerics were not so zealous. The ninth century Bishops of Lyons, Agobard, and Amulo sought to sever the happy relationship between Jews and gentiles as they denounced "Jewish insolence." Church leaders, bishops, abbots, and theologians launched their missiles against Judaism in every conceivable fashion.

Jews were lepers, said Ambrose and Theodoret.

Jews were economic exploiters and venal usurers, declared Peter of Cluny and Bernard of Clairvaux.

Jews were perfidious misanthropes who could not be trusted and ought be kept at a distance from the faithful.

Jews were lascivious.

Jews were aligned with Satan and possessed demonic powers; they were "children of Lucifer."

Jews were black magicians.

Jews poisoned wells and spread the plague.

Jews were engaged in an international conspiracy to subvert Christendom.

Jews desecrated the host.

Jews killed Christian children and used their blood for unleavened bread.

Gentle, saintly Bernard of Clairvaux was no better. True, he chided rabble-rousing Radulph, the ignorant pogromist monk of the Second Crusade, saying that Jews ought to be won over by arguments rather than arms. But Bernard also wrote anti-Jewish poems. And he denounced Pope Anacletes II (a descendant of Jews) as "immersed in night of perfidy" like all other Jews. Bernard wrote that the Jews "are the living sign to us, representing the Lord's Passion. For this reason they are dispersed to all regions, that they may be the witnesses of our redemption." And he added that they are "a race who had not God for their faith, but were of the devil, and were murderers."

In art, music, literature, and theatre, Jews were painted in the blackest light. The great Strasbourg Cathedral depicts a disheveled, blindfolded woman—symbol of the vanquished synagogue. Nearby is a statue of a proud, handsome, crowned woman—symbol of the Church triumphant. Jews were often depicted with horns on their heads; sometimes they appeared beneath the symbol of a scorpion. In music, their role is equally black (*viz.*, Bach's great chorales). In the theatre, the usurer Shylock demanding a pound of flesh is fixed in our minds. The Byzantine dramas of Romanos and the Passion plays have always been anti-Jewish. In literature, the nefarious, well-poisoner and devil's-sire Jew has been preserved in every western language.

Such conditioning could only lead to violence, as indeed it did with the Crusades.

The Crusades mark the great turning point in medieval Judeo-Christian relations. In the name of God, with pectoral crosses adorning their breasts, the Crusaders drenched their swords in Jewish blood in France, Germany, England and Jerusalem. Led by Peter the Hermit, the rabble of the First Crusade marched to this tune:

> *We are marching a great distance to seek our sanc-*
> *tuary and to take vengeance on the Muslims. Lo and*
> *behold, there live among us Jews whose forefathers*
> *slew Him [Jesus] and crucified Him for no cause. Let*
> *us revenge ourselves on them first and eliminate them*
> *from among the nations, so that the name of Israel no*
> *longer be remembered, or else let them be like our-*
> *selves and believe in the son of Mary.*

Once again, the text most favored by the Crusaders was Matthew 27:25. It was believed meritorious to shed the blood of the infidel Jew. As Radulph preached in the days of the Second Crusade, "Jews residing in hamlets and cities ought to be killed as enemies of the Christian faith."

From this point on, Jews were no longer safe; psychologically and physically, their status was impaired. Three days were set forth each year in Barcelona, Marseilles, and Florence for assault and plundering in the Jewish quarter. In Toulouse, at Easter time, a public slap to the face was given the leading Jew—a custom replaced in the twelfth century by a tax for the clergy.

In Béziers, permission was given on the eve of Palm Sunday and during the following two weeks to stone the Jewish quarter. And Easter Sunday—with its Passion motif in which the Jews were graphically depicted as deicides and lynchers—was often the spark that touched off pogroms in Eastern and Western Europe.

Bloody riots were also precipitated by hideous and nonsensical libels. Jews were condemned for desecrating the Host and making it bleed, or cry. And each time, lives were lost because of that disgraceful nonsense. Even worse was the sordid blood libel. Jews were accused of killing a Christian child and using his blood to bake *matzot* for the Passover. The first such libel was at Norwich in 1144. An entire cult honoring the boy William sprang up. In Blois, 1171, fifty-one Jews paid with their lives. The libel concerning Little Hugh of Lincoln in 1255, cost the Jews nineteen killed. Simon of Trent's murder in 1475 led to the total annihilation of that Jewish community.

As recently as 1928, in Massena, New York, ritual blood libels have cropped up. And it is rumored that in the Soviet Union till this day, blood libels are extant, and Jews are innocent victims.

True, the Papacy generally condemned these outrages (apart from Innocent III who accepted their validity) and issued Bulls denouncing such libels. But only as recently as October 31, 1965, did the Catholic Church officially exonerate the Jews of Trent of the murder of Simon in 1475 and admit that "a judicial assassination" had taken place. And never did the Papacy truly bridle the local clerics or masses in this sordid matter.

In view of this mass of evidence—only a fraction of the facts—it is difficult to comprehend how Francis Cardinal Spellman could have possibly declared in a speech to the American Jewish Committee on April 30, 1964, that he was "appalled" that so many Christians attributed the suffering of the Jews to their part in the Crucifixion. "This is not Christianity. I don't know where they learned it, but surely it was not from the teachings of their church. . . . Anti-Semitism can never find a basis in the Catholic religion."

Such a statement simply flies in the face of nineteen centuries of reality.

The balance sheet of the Protestant Church has not been much more exemplary. True, in the long run Jews fared better under Protestantism than under Catholicism except, of course, in Germany. But Protestant sects, especially the fundamentalist groups, have been and still are profoundly anti-Semitic. The Eastern Orthodox Churches sanctioned Cossack massacres and pogroms; their priests blessed murderers about to imbrue their hands in Jewish blood. Pobiedonotsev, Procurator of the Holy Russian Synod and confidant of Czar Alexander III, suggested this solution to the Jewish question: One third will emigrate, one third convert, and one third will perish. Even the Negro churches, recalls Richard Wright wistfully, instilled religious anti-Semitism in their adherents by branding Jews "deicides" in their Sunday Schools and pulpits. Negro anti-Semitism is, essentially, no different from the white version.

Of course, Protestant anti-Semitism derives from its ancient and medieval roots in the Gospels and in Catholic doctrine. But the great Protestant reformers of the sixteenth century were also decidedly anti-Semitic. Zwingli reiterated the Church's assertation that since Jesus, Christians have become the New Israel, and the Jews have degenerated into Gentile people. Calvin burned Servetus because of his "judaizing" anti-Trinitarianism, while Servetus denounced Calvinistic legalism as Jewish.

None of the Protestant reformers exceeded Martin Luther, however, in vitriolic, obscene anti-Semitism. At first, Luther was kindly disposed towards Jews, hoping thereby to convert them to Christianity. He wrote that were he a Jew he would rather suffer ten times the most terrible of deaths than join the papacy, but like Mohammed, he was soon disillusioned. When Jews spurned his campaign of reform, he became—again like Mohammed—a violent Jew-baiter. Here are some typical statements:

*There is no people under the sun so avid of revenge,
so blood thirsty, believing itself to be God's people
merely in order to strangle and immolate the heathens.*

*Know, Christians, that next to the devil thou hast no
enemy more cruel, more venomous and violent than a
true Jew.*

Luther accused the Jews of all the old crimes attributed
to them by the Catholic Church—usury, well-poisoning,
ritual murder, black magic. . . . He urged the princes to
burn their synagogues and "threaten to tear their tongues
from their throats if they do not accept the Christian proof
that God is three and not one." And he instigated the German princes to banish them unless they would convert.
One of his foulest passages, a passage worthy of pornogra-
pher Julius Streicher, admonishes the Jews that "the only
Bible you have any right to is that concealed beneath the
sow's tail; the letters that drop from it you are free to eat
and drink." In equally edifying language Luther preached
that "the Devil, with his angelic snout, devours what
exudes from the oral and anal apertures of the Jews; this is
indeed his favorite dish, on which he battens like a sow
behind the hedge. . . ."

Thus spoke the founder of Protestantism. And thus
taught the man who, as William L. Shirer points out,
shaped so much of the thinking of modern Germany. He
taught Germany absolute obedience to the leader and state.
And he taught his father land foul hatred for the Jew. . . .

That German Protestantism aided and abetted the rise of
the Third Reich is an incontrovertable and tragic fact. All
churches, writes William L. Shirer, welcomed Hitler and
the Nazis. The Reverend Ludwig Mueller formed the

Nazi "German Christian Faith Movement" and by 1933 he had enrolled three thousand out of seventeen thousand Protestant pastors as members. Pastor Martin Niemöller welcomed the New Order—including its anti-Jewish policies. Only when Hitler's fury turned on the former U-Boat Captain did Niemöller have a change of heart.

Bishop Otto Dibelius, the most respected leader of the German Evangelical Church, preached to his flock: "In spite of the ugly sound often attached to the word, I have always regarded myself as an anti-Semite. The fact cannot be concealed that the Jews have played a leading part in the disintegration of modern civilization."

Bishop Marahrens of Hanover urged all Protestant pastors to swear a personal oath of allegiance to the Fuehrer. All did so in 1937 and 1938. Martin Luther's venom found full expression in his Protestant heirs of the twentieth century. German Protestants were pro-Nazi, anti-Jewish, and therefore accomplices to mass murder.

The record of German Catholics is just as dismal and the more reprehensible in view of the authority and respect enjoyed by the hierarchy. Professor Guenter Lewy agrees with Jules Isaac that without centuries of Christian preaching and teaching, the "Final Solution" of the Jewish question would not have been possible. Every aspect of German Catholicism, like German Protestantism, was saturated with venom against Jews.

The Catholic population of Germany was 43.1 per cent in 1939; 22.7 per cent of the S.S. were Catholics. Long before Hitler's rise to power in 1933, German Catholicism was continuing the medieval legacy of Church-sponsored anti-Semitism.

For centuries the Passion Play had been presented at Oberammergau. In 1960, some 400,000 people saw this play of Christian religious fervor. Professor Robert Davies observed that even after the war, Jews in the play were depicted as dark, sly, conniving Christ-killers, while the Christians are played by tall, blond Aryans. And in Deggendorf, a pageant depicting the Blood Libel of 1337 was repeated annually until 1960, when 10,000 were in attendance for the last performance of that canard.

Before the advent of Hitler, Catholic Bishops urged Germans to defend themselves against Jewish capitalists. Others were equally vehement in warning about Jewish Bolshevism. Curate Roth preached that innocent as well as guilty Jews would have to suffer on the day of reckoning, and Father Bernhard Sempfle, a Catholic priest and anti-Semitic journalist, helped Hitler edit *Mein Kampf*. When Hitler rose to the Chancelorship, Germany's three Cardinals—Bertram, Faulhaber, and Schulte—and twenty bishops and archbishops were solidly in his camp, as were also the churchmen of Catholic Austria.

In 1933, Cardinal Faulhaber delivered a series of advent sermons in which he defended the Old Testament against its detractors, but he made it clear that he was *not* defending Jews who lived after the death of Jesus. These were doomed to be restless wanderers on earth even to the present day. When a false sermon was circulated that purported to defend Jews against racialism, Faulhaber quickly disavowed it.

In 1939, Archbishop Gröber and Bishop Hilfrich of Limberg condemned Jews as deicides. Pilate, they said was an Aryan; the Jews were all Semitic Judases. In March 1941, Gröber again blamed the Jews for the crucifixion and declared that the curse of Matthew 27:25 "has come true, terribly true until the present time, until today."

The Church remained silent even in the face of the most

ghoulish pogroms. After the *Kristallnacht* of November, 1938, when 191 synagogues were set on fire, 76 others destroyed, 36 Jews killed and 20,000 male Jews arrested and sent to concentration camps, Provost Lichtenberg alone raised his voice in protest. Yet the Church fiercely denounced the euthanasia campaign directed against mental defectives and, in fact, put a stop to that abomination in 1941. The Church fought successfully to protect so-called non-Aryan Catholics (*i.e.*, Catholics of Jewish descent or birth who were condemned as non-Aryans by the Nuremburg Laws).

By the end of 1942, the Episcopate knew *all* about the "Final Solution," yet it opposed tyrannicide and urged obedience to the *Fuehrer*. Only a handful of courageous priests—among them Delp, Reinisch, and Lichtenberg— spoke out against Nazi atrocities and laid down their lives in the process. All this happened when the Catholic churches of Holland, Belgium, and France *did* speak out and act to save Jews, and while Danish and Norwegian pastors were risking their lives to shelter and protect their Jewish neighbors. Gordon Zahn concludes that "in World War II, the leading spokesmen of the Catholic Church in Germany did become channels of Nazi control over their followers, whether by their general exhortations to loyal obedience to legitimate authority, or by their even more direct efforts to rally these followers to the defense of *Volk*, *Vaterland*, and *Heimat* as a Christian duty." And to quote Guenter Lewy once more: "The Church, custodian of Christian love and charity stood by silently."

Of all the painful indictments of Christianity over its failure to save Jews in World War II, however, none is more controversial than that concerning the Vatican. Ever since the presentation of Rolf Hochhuth's play, *The Deputy*, the guilt of Pope Pius XII has become an international issue for debate. True, the Pope worked behind the scenes in purchasing exit visas and in sheltering Jews in monasteries, hospices, and nunneries. In Rome, 4,447 Jewish citizens were thus saved in 1943. But the Pope, who was pro-German, violently anti-Communist, and an ardent "neutralist," never condemned Nazi extermination programs. He never excommunicated Catholic mass murderers and criminals. In 124 letters written to the German bishops from 1939 to 1944, he referred to the Jews only *once*, when he recalled to Bishop von Preysing of Berlin that he had spent large amounts in American currency for visas. But there was no word of exhortation to aid Jews, no word of condemnation for genocide, no admonition to Polish Bishops that Jews were to be protected from the liquidation program, of which he knew by the end of 1942. He uttered no public excoriation, despite the urging of the Allies, Jewish leaders, and Catholic prelates. He made no outcry when eight thousand Roman Jews were rounded up for deportation beneath his very window in October, 1943. . . .

In 1940, Cardinal Tisserant vainly begged Pius XII to condemn Nazism. After the pontiff's rebuff, Tisserant wrote prophetically, "I fear that history will reproach the Holy See with having practiced a policy of selfish convenience and not much else." And in Albert Schweitzer's words, although both Protestant and Catholic churches are guilty in the slaughter of Europe's Jews, the Catholic Church must bear greater guilt because "it was an organized, supra-national power in a position to do something. . . ."

Pius XII abandoned the traditional (albeit half-hearted) policy of papal protection over Jewry. The price was ghastly. The Pope violated one of the Bible's most profound commandments: "Thou shall not stand idly by while thy neighbor's blood is being shed." [7]

The "harvest of hate" (to borrow Léon Poliakov's phrase) was reaped in the "Final Solution" of the Jewish problem in World War II with the extermination of six million Jews.

How could it have happened?

Let James Parkes, eminent Anglican minister and scholar speak:

In our own day . . . more than six million deliberate murders are the consequence of the teachings about Jews for which the Christian Church is ultimately responsible . . . its ultimate resting place is in the teaching of the New Testament itself.

Let Professor Guenter Lewy speak:

Without centuries of Christian catechism, preaching, and vituperations, the Hitlerian teachings, propaganda, and vituperation would not have been possible.

Let Professor Helmut Krausnick of the Munich Institute of Modern History speak:

Adolph Hitler was not an accident but the result of centuries of anti-Semitism in Germany.

And let the great existentialist philosopher Jean Paul Sartre (in the idiom of that malevolent verse in Matthew 27:25) speak:

The Jewish blood shed by the Nazis is upon the heads of all of us.

On all of us, yes!

It is on the heads of the British leaders who refused to open the gates of Palestine to Jewish refugees.

It is on the heads of an American government that preserved immigration quotas when thousands were hammering on the gates to leave Hell.

It is on the heads of the British and American Generals who refused to bomb railroad lines leading to death camps and gas chambers and crematoria within those infernos because of "technical difficulties."

It is on the heads of an American State Department that refused to raise or transfer ransom money ($1,000 per family to be deposited in Swiss banks) to buy Jews from their murderers.

It is on the head of Admiral William D. Leahy, President Roosevelt's Chief of Staff, who rejected a plan (April 26, 1943) to move Jewish refugees from Europe to North Africa because "the influx . . . might cause such resentment on the part of the Arab population as to necessitate military action to maintain order," and because it would impose "added and unwarranted administrative responsibility on the supreme commander in North Africa."

It is on the head of British Colonial Secretary, Lord Moyne, who responded to Adolph Eichmann's proposal of trucks for Jews with his, "But where shall I put a million Jews?"

But above all, it is on the head of the churches—Catholic and Protestant—who prepared the soil and implanted the seeds of hatred in men's hearts so that they felt no compunctions at shooting or gassing Jews, no remorse that their borders remained closed to refugees clutching for straws.

Hitler had been born a Catholic. He was educated at a Benedictine Monastery at Lambach for two years. He even dreamed of taking holy orders.[8]

Rudolph Hoess, who, as commandant of Auschwitz, admitted to killing over 3 million victims, had a similar pious Catholic background.

Franz Von Pappen was so staunch a Catholic that Pope Pius XII made him a Papal Chamberlain *after* the War!

Eichmann was raised in a religious Protestant home in Linz, Austria.

And none of these fiends were ever excommunicated or read out of their churches. Nor did Catholic or Protestant churches speak out against the murder of Jews in clear and unequivocal terms.

No, the calamity of the 6 million was no accident.

One wonders how often Eichmann or Hitler or Himmler heard their parents speak of the "Christ-killers" and the accursed Jews who rejected the Savior? How many times did those phrases resound in the young and impressionable ears of future Nazis (as they had in the ears of millions of other children for centuries), conditioning them unconsciously, if not consciously, to hate the Jews who had "sold out Germany" as they had "sold out the Lord" nineteen centuries before?

How many Nazis and S.S. men were conditioned like Pavlov's dogs, in Sunday Schools, in churches, or simply at the family table, especially at Easter or Christmas, to bristle with hostility and hatred at the very mention of the name "Jew?" Consciously and unconsciously, through direction and indirection, the mark of Cain has been branded on our heads.

And who will expunge that mark? Who will make amends? Who will close the wounds of hate and bring healing to the "daughter of my People?"

Who, indeed, if not the churches of Christendom. . . .

NOTES

1 Luke 23:34
2 Genesis 27:40
3 Salo W. Baron, *A Social and Religious History of the Jews*, Vol. X
4 Gregory, *Sicut Judaeis*, analyzed in Solomon Grayzel's, *The*
Church and the Jews in the XlIIth Century, pp. 9 ff.
5 Genesis 27:40
6 Cf. Galatians 4:30
7 Leviticus 19:16
8 Adolf Hitler, *Mein Kampf*, p. 6

IX

Ecumenism and Judeo-Christian Dialogue

"Then those who feared the Lord spoke together."

MALACHI 3:16

No religious event in recent decades has stirred the souls of men more profoundly than the Ecumenical Council Vatican II. The eyes of the entire world—not just the Catholic world—were focused on Rome for the duration of the lengthy sessions of the first Ecumenical Council held in a century. The Council had been summoned by the late and lamented Pope John XXIII and it was concluded under his successor, Pope Paul VI, and its world-wide impact will be felt for many, many years.

The word "ecumenical," and its cognates, "ecumenism," "ecumenicity," derive from the Greek *oikumene,* meaning "world-wide, universal." Thus, the idea of the ecumenical movement is to unite all of Christendom beneath one banner. In the case of the Ecumenical Council Vatican II, the banner beneath which all Christendom was to rally was the fleur-de-lys of the Pope in Rome, but the Council in Rome had a second purpose in mind. John

XXIII convened it, he said, in order to let some fresh air into the Church in an attempt (as he put it) at *aggiorna-mento*—"updating the Roman Catholic faith." Unquestionably there was such a need. Since the last such council held in 1870, the entire world had changed. And religion had to change apace.

Actually, the ecumenical movement had begun years before in Protestant circles. Leaders of the Protestant groups have been deeply concerned over the atomization of their faith (there are over 250 Protestant sects in America alone!) and they have been urging the unification of their groups into one, universal church. But none of the ecumenical attempts of the Protestant groups captured world attention as did the Catholic Council in Rome.

The drive for unity is not the sole purpose of the ecumenical stirrings. There is an even more crucial reason. The Christian groups are concerned over the loss of the faithful and the decline of church influence since World War II. Nazism shattered the church; Communism has all but crushed Eastern Orthodoxy and Catholicism; Islam is winning out in Africa; Asia has either gone Communist or has remained indifferent to missionizing efforts. The three great "isms"—"atheism," "Communism," and "materialism"—have challenged Christianity as never before.

There is yet one more reason behind ecumenical stirrings: the churches of Christendom are lacerated with a sense of guilt. Christianity died at Auschwitz for many Europeans; Asians buried it at Hiroshima; Africans have spurned it in South Africa, for all of the unspeakable crimes perpetrated in these varied locales have been perpetrated by so-called "Christian" nations—with barely perceptible protests from priests and clerics.

For all of these reasons, then, churchmen and theologians have been undergoing unprecedented and unusually frank soul-searching and self-examination. Every facet of human problems, of moral dilemmas, of theological concepts are being passed under the microscope of doubt. In the process, the relationship of Christianity to Judaism has also been re-examined.

Why? Because Christianity realizes that it is partly, if not primarily, responsible for the tragedy of the Jews in our times. It knows now that it prepared the soil for the annihilation of 6 million Jews, including over a million children. It realizes, too, that the voices of protest of moral leaders and religious spokesmen were strangely muffled at a time when mankind's conscience cried out for some reproval. Yes, Christendom finally has been moved to make amends, to reach out for Judaism and say, "Forgive me, brother!"

In view of this failure of man and institution, it is not difficult to understand why Protestant and Catholic circles have sought to correct historic injustices towards the Jewish People.

Vatican II encompassed many areas of human life and thought. The section of the Schema dealing with the Jews was only a small part of a vast number of debates, studies, and pronunciamentos, yet it achieved world-wide notoriety far out of proportion to the time allotted it in the Council's deliberations. Perhaps that is due to the Church's uneasy conscience over the matter; perhaps it is because no other Schema was as bitterly contested.

At any rate, I believe that the Schema dealing with the Jews would never have been inserted had it not been for one warm, humanitarian, loving man—Pope John XXIII. It was he who insisted the Augustin Cardinal Bea study the question of Judeo-Catholic relations; it was he who insisted that the Council place it on its agenda. What a pity that he did not live to see the final vote and the fruition of his dream!

Why was Pope John so intent on including a section on the Jews? He doubtlessly bore scars of guilt—guilt over his predecessor's failure to speak out and unequivocally condemn Nazi atrocities, for John knew first-hand how the Papacy had failed. While he was Papal Nuncio in Turkey, Archbishop Roncalli (the future Pope John) petitioned Pius XII to grant an audience to Chief Rabbi Herzog of the Holy Land in order to discuss the question of Nazi extermination camps (1943). The Pope refused. In the same year Roncalli also asked for an audience with Pius in order to arrange to save several hundred Jewish children in Bratislavia, Czechoslavakia. The Pope would not grant an audience, and the children. . . . The children ended up in gas chambers. So John realized how the Papacy had been an accomplice, albeit silent, to the "Final Solution." As Nuncio, he had tried his best. Sally Mayer, director of rescue operations for Jews in Europe, recalls that Roncalli had been a true humanitarian. He had helped obtain visas and false papers for Jewish refugees from Rumania. No doubt his firsthand experiences with the holocaust moved John XXIII to action at the highest level.

There was one other factor, I think, that impelled John on his mission of conciliation and re-examination of Judeo-Christian relations. Scholars and churchmen throughout the world sought to compel that re-examination. Catholic layman Malcolm Hay and Angelican Minister James Parkes were struggling for it in England; Reinhold Niebuhr and

James Pike were demanding it in America; Protestant circles were already deep in the problem; and a frail, scholarly professor in France—Jules Isaac—was determined to achieve results on the highest level. All were appalled at the holocaust; all were convinced that the churches had paved the way, and had not yet made amends.

Jules Isaac launched a private campaign to pluck out the religious roots of anti-Semitism. He had convened private conferences after the war to re-evaluate religious textbooks; he had vainly urged Pius XII to take action. But in John XXIII he found a listening ear and a discerning eye, in addition to a tender heart. John was impressed; he realized that his Papacy must make amends, and he acted. In 1959 he removed the adjective "perfidious" from the age-old Good Friday prayer, *pro perfidis Judaeis*. And more: the Pope appointed Augustin Cardinal Bea, a German Jesuit, to study the problem of anti-Semitism and to formulate a section in the Schema on relations with non-Catholics that would eternally condemn anti-Semitism and lift the curse of deicide from Jewish shoulders. The declaration of the Jews was in the works, but it would not be simple to pass it.

The Ecumenical Council's action on the Jewish People resembled a theological tennis match. The positions shifted from the liberals to the conservatives and back again. At the very outset it appeared that a fiasco was in the offing. Dr. Nahum Goldmann, President of the World Jewish Congress, announced that he had been invited as an official observer. A hue and cry promptly arose from religious quarters. Then it was announced that an Israeli, Dr. Haim Vardi, would be present in behalf of world Jewry (July,

1962). Immediately the Arabs protested. Both the American Jewish Committee and the B'nai Brith sought not only to drive home their messages in the chambers of the Vatican, but also to capture headlines and credits. The jockeying and maneuvering were neither entirely reputable nor savory.

Still, the first session was presented with a strong draft statement in line with Jules Isaac's suggestions and Pope John's thinking (November 8, 1963). The proposal reaffirmed the Jewish roots of Christianity. It then noted that the responsibility for the death of Jesus falls on the shoulders of sinful mankind, not just the Jews. The personal guilt of those Jewish leaders who demanded the death of Jesus surely cannot be attributed to all Jews, then or now. Hence, it is unjust to brand Jews "deicide." The proposal also admonished preachers and teachers never to present a contrary position that might give rise to hatred. Finally, as a means of assuaging prelates in Moslem lands, the proposed Schema stressed that it was purely a religious document and that it could not be called pro-Zionist because the Schema was not a political text.

Matters were by no means simple and conclusive. The Conservative and Arab prelates rallied, and the document was temporarily shelved to be voted on at the second session. Before the second session, tragedy struck: John XXIII died—to the consternation of the free world and the dismay of men of good will.

In the interim, the anti-Semites, the Conservatives, and the Arab-land prelates joined forces. Cardinal Ruffini decried "honorable mention of Jews," and he queried, "Why not consider religions less hostile to the Church?"

Cardinal Appouri and the Middle Eastern prelates warned that the position of the faithful in Moslem lands would suffer.

The position of the new Pope, Paul VI, was either ambiguous, or worse, hostile to the Jews. Either he himself believed the deicide charge and allowed the shelving or dilution of the statement, or he rejected the charge but was afraid to offend the Curia and conservative prelates. His position is unclear to this day.

At any rate, more shocks and machinations were ahead. On September 4, 1964, a frankly missionizing, watered-down version of the Schema was leaked to the press. The text called for "the reunion of the Jewish people with the Church" and it deleted the phrase "deicide." It also reminded preachers and teachers to refrain from "accusing Jews of our times what was perpetrated during the passion of the Christ."

Now it was the turn of the Jewish community to howl. Many who had been wary were crushed; others tauntingly reproved the Jewish ambassadors with "I told you so." Three American Rabbinical groups denounced toadyism and *shtadlanut* (flunky-like diplomacy). Professor Abraham J. Heschel flew to Rome to see the Pope and closeted himself in with Bea.

Remarkably, however, the liberal churchmen themselves rallied. Ritter, Meyer, and Cushing of the United States, joined forces with Heenan of England and Suenans of Belgium. Boston's gravel-voiced Cardinal Cushing delivered an eloquent appeal (September 28) in which he declared: "First, we must make our statement about the Jews more positive, less timid, more charitable." Said the late President John F. Kennedy's personal chaplain: ". . . We must deny

that the Jews are guilty of the death of our Saviour. . . .
And especially, we must condemn any who would attempt
to justify inequities, hatred, or even persecution of the
Jews as Christian actions." Finally, in a frank confession of
guilt, Cushing rebuked his apathetic colleagues for their
inactivity during the holocaust:

> *I ask . . . whether we ought not to confess humbly
> before the world that Christians too frequently have
> not shown themselves as true Christians . . . in their
> relations with their Jewish brothers? In this age, how
> many have suffered! How many have died because of
> the indifference of Christians, because of silence!
> . . . If not many Christian voices were lifted in re-
> cent years against the great injustices, yet let our
> voices humbly cry out now.*

Finally, after four years and much wrangling, maneuvering, back-room politicking, and recriminations, the Council
voted on October 15, 1965 by 1,763 to 250 to pass the
section on the Jews as part of the Schema "On the Relations of the Church to Non-Christian Religions," and on
October 28 Pope Paul promulgated it.

Pope John's dream was fulfilled. True, it did not contain
the original liberal text that stated, "All that happened to
Christ in His passion cannot be attributed to the whole
people then alive, much less to those of today." Neither did
it emphatically "condemn" hatred and persecution and urge
preachers, teachers, and catechetical writers never to
"present the Jewish people as one rejected, cursed, or
guilty of deicide" or "teach anything that could give rise to
hatred or contempt of Jews in the hearts of Christians," as

the former text read. In fact, the word "deicide" was dropped and the strong "condemn" was replaced with the flaccid "deplore"—allegedly because the Church only "condemns" *heresies* (although in March, 1928, the Holy See *did* "condemn" anti-Semitism). I suspect that the change was Pope Paul's, for in a speech to American Jewish leaders (May 30, 1964) he used the words: ". . . we again strongly deplore the horrible ordeals of which the Jews have been the victims in recent years. . . ." On the other hand, the final statement adds the word "anti-Semitism."

Still, it is undeniable that the final version marks a compromise with the conservatives and bigots over the originally accepted draft Schema. There are loopholes and ambiguities, and there is lacking a firm and final condemnation of the deicide charge and a disavowal of the teaching of contempt and the system of degradation that had marred Judeo-Christian relations for centuries. In its final form, the section on the Jews reads:

> *As this Sacred Synod searches into the mystery of the Church, it remembers the bond that spiritually ties the people of the New Covenant to Abraham's stock.*
>
> *Thus, the Church of Christ acknowledges that, according to God's saving design, the beginnings of her faith and her election are found already among the Patriarchs, Moses and the prophets. She professes that all who believe in Christ—Abraham's sons, according to faith—are included in the same Patriarch's call, and likewise that the salvation of the Church is mysteriously foreshadowed by the chosen people's exodus from the land of bondage. The Church, there-*

fore, cannot forget that she received the revelation of the Old Testament through the people with whom God in His inexpressible mercy concluded the Ancient Covenant. Nor can she forget that she draws sustenance from the root of that well-cultivated olive tree onto which have been grafted the wild shoots, the Gentiles. Indeed, the Church believes that by His cross Christ Our Peace reconciled Jews and Gentiles, making both one in Himself.

The Church keeps ever in mind the words of the Apostle about his kinsmen: 'theirs is the sonship and the glory and the covenants and the law and the worship and the promises; theirs are the fathers, and from them is the Christ according to the flesh,' [1] the Son of the Virgin Mary. She also recalls that the Apostles, the Church's mainstay and pillars, as well as most of the early disciples who proclaimed Christ's Gospel to the world, sprang from the Jewish people.

As Holy Scripture testifies, Jerusalem did not recognize the time of her visitation, nor did the Jews, in large number, accept the Gospel, indeed not a few opposed its spreading. Nevertheless, God holds the Jews most dear for the sake of their fathers; He does not repent of the gifts He makes or of the calls He issues—such is the witness of the Apostle. In company with the prophets and the same Apostle, the Church awaits the day, known to God alone, on which all peoples will address the Lord in a single voice and "serve him shoulder to shoulder." [2]

Since the spiritual patrimony common to Christians and Jews is thus so great, this Sacred Synod wants to *foster and recommend that mutual understanding and respect which is the fruit, above all, of Biblical and theological studies as well as of fraternal dialogues.*

True, the Jewish authorities and those who followed their lead pressed for the death of Christ; still, what happened in His passion cannot be charged against all the Jews, without distinction, then alive, nor against the Jews of today. Although the Church is the new people of God, the Jews should not be presented as rejected by God or accursed, as if this followed from the Holy Scriptures. All should see to it, then, that in catechetical work or in the preaching of the word of God they do not teach anything that does not conform to the truth of the Gospel and the spirit of Christ.

Furthermore, in her rejection of every persecution against any man, the Church, mindful of the patrimony she shares with the Jews and moved not by political reasons but by the Gospel's spiritual love, decries hatred, persecutions, displays of anti-Semitism, directed against Jews at any time and by anyone.

Besides, as the Church has always held and holds now, Christ underwent His passion and death freely, because of the sins of men and out of infinite love, in order that all may reach salvation. It is, therefore, the burden of the Church's preaching to proclaim the cross of Christ as the sign of God's all-embracing love and as the fountain from which every grace flows.

The Council Schema on the Jews did not go as far as it might have gone, but it was a beginning. In the words of Richard Cardinal Cushing: ". . . the statement is only a beginning for us to go further and to take out of Christian literature all that reflects upon the Jewish people. . . . The declaration we have is not perfect, but, in my opinion, it is a good start."

It will not be easy to eradicate nineteen centuries of hatred. Pope Paul himself illustrated that truth during the deliberations themselves. In a Lenten mass held on Passion Sunday, the Pope delivered a homily on John 7:45-59. He called the day "a grave and sad page because it narrates the conflict, the clash between Jesus and the Hebrew people, a people predestined to await the Messiah but who, just at the right moment, not only did not recognize Him but fought Him, abused Him and finally killed Him."

Incredibly, even after the final vote and promulgation of the Schema on the Jews, Bishop Luigi Carli of Segni, Italy, wrote a forty-four-page article in a clerical review *Palestro del Clero* in which he stated that Judaism "by its very nature carries the judgment of condemnation by God." Carli concluded that ". . . whoever knowing Christ, consciously and freely adheres to Judaism, participates in conscience in that judgment of condemnation." Old stereotypes and prejudices die slowly, it appears.

Protestant churches are finding the same pitfalls to change. The churches of the Protestant sects had anticipated the Vatican by adopting statements absolving the Jews of the deicide charge and condemning anti-Semitism. The World Council of Churches at New Delhi in 1961, the National Council of Churches of Christ in America in 1964, the Lutheran World Federation in April, 1964, and the Protestant Episcopal House of Bishops in October of 1964 all adopted such resolutions. And yet, fundamentalist groups still spew forth hatred and anti-Semitic stereotypes, and images remain even among groups that have disavowed such attitudes.

The newly published study of anti-Semitic attitudes conducted at the University of California at Los Angeles for the B'nai Brith has clearly demonstrated how much work remains to be done. Briefly, the study disclosed that the religious roots of anti-Semitism are very deep. In fact, only 5 per cent of the anti-Semites studied seemed to have *no* religious motivation. Among Protestants, 33 per cent showed high or medium high anti-Semitic feelings; among Catholics, the degree was 29 per cent. The more fundamentalist sects (*e.g.*, Southern Baptists, Missouri Synod Lutherans, etc.) displayed the highest percentage of anti-Semitic sentiments. Furthermore, the Jews were generally implicated in the crucifixion story, and that belief "provides an important basis for generating hostile religious images of the modern Jews." In fact, 43 per cent of the Protestants and 50 per cent of the Roman Catholics blamed the Jews for the crucifixion.

In view of the foregoing study, what can be done to expunge prejudicial attitudes? How can the ecumenical movement's pronouncements on the Jews and anti-Semitism be implemented?

Au fond, a theological shift and change in emphasis must be made by Christian groups. The concept of deicide, while not an official dogma of the churches, must be expunged forever. The idea of the accursed, wandering Jew must be obliterated. And the gory depiction of the crucifixion must be reinterpreted so as not to label any group as murderers. Surely, one cannot teach his child that the boy next door murdered his God and expect love and fraternity to reign. Such theological reevaluations have been made before: they must be made again if there is to be any hope of fraternity and religious peace.

Secondly, passages in Scripture and Patristic literature and liturgy that generate Jew-hatred and mar happy inter-religious relations ought to be removed or avoided. In the case of Scripture this is difficult, since Christians view their Bible as sacred literature, the word of God Himself. But preachers need not choose the most anti-Semitic texts for sermons or liturgy, and textbook authors must not select such Biblical passages for use in shaping malleable minds. We Jews have taken the step: prayers that gave offense to Christians have been deleted or reworded; passages in the Talmud have been censored. And we no longer utilize Biblical texts that have lost relevance for today. No rabbi would suggest that witches be burned, or Sabbath violators be stoned. Nor would Jewish preachers select less edifying or barbaric sections of the Bible for homiletical material and insertion in the Prayer Book. Sensitive selectivity is required of church leaders.

Thirdly, the entire educational system of Christendom on all levels will have to be revised. Texts used in Sunday and parochial schools must be examined and scrutinized lest they plant the malevolent seeds in young minds. Similarly, texts used in training priests, nuns, ministers, and religious teachers must be corrected to conform to the idea of human brotherhood and mutual respect. Studies of religious texts are now being conducted in the United States, Belgium, and Latin America. They have disclosed the appalling fact that textbooks used in parochial and Sunday schools and in adult education still perpetuate the myth of the accursed, deicide people. Here are some examples chosen at random from children's texts in English, French, and Spanish.

> *The Jews wanted to disgrace Christ by having Him die on the cross.*
>
> *The Jews as a nation refused to accept Christ, and since that time have been wandering on the earth without a temple or a sacrifice and without the Messias.*
>
> *The punishment of the deicide Jews was not long delayed. Thirty-six years after the Saviour's death, the Roman Emperor Titus captured Jerusalem and utterly destroyed the Jewish temple. The Jews, dispersed throughout the world, have never been able to become once more a nation. They have wandered about, regarded as an accursed race, as an object of contempt to other peoples.*

A primer used in Spain for first graders today shows Jews crucifying a Spanish Christian child postured on a wall like Jesus with a halo on his head. The primer then queries: "Of what Biblical incident does this story remind you?"

A Protestant text used in America reads:

> *They [the Jews] were so filled with hatred for Him that they shouted themselves hoarse crying: "Crucify Him!" That was the thanks He received for coming into this world to save and bless them.*

Another Sunday school text asks this test question: "Give proof that the curse which the Jews called down upon their nation still rests upon them and their children even to this very day." I can imagine some eager, bright, ten-year old raising his hand and saying: "The murder of the six million Jews is the best proof of that fact, teacher."

Summarizing studies of Catholic and Protestant texts done at St. Louis and Yale Universities, Bishop James Pike wrote that "the sad and shocking fact is that the roots of bias often reach back to the pulpit and the Sunday school class; the seeds of hatred frequently are planted by the churches themselves by what they teach, what they fail to teach, and what they are." The former Dean of Union Theological Seminary, Dr. John Bennett, agrees that "religious conditioning prepares [the children] for a negative attitude towards Jews. . . . The religious roots of anti-Semitism are still important in this country." And Dr. Bernhard Olsen found that while Protestant texts condemn prejudice *per se,* invariably anti-Catholic and anti-Jewish prejudice creeps into history and theology lessons by both what is said and what is unsaid. Explosive phrases that never fail to conjure up visions of perfidy such as "popists," "Christ-killers," and "Pharisees and hypocrites" are frequently used. Consequently, Jews are branded as Christ-killers and are held collectively responsible for his death. Jesus no longer appears as a Jew; his mortal enemies are the perfidious Jews—he is depicted as an innocent Christian martyr. And Pontius Pilate (that repacious murderer!) is depicted as a "saint," while the Jews are damned for having "blinded" themselves to the truth by their rejection of the "Saviour," and must suffer eternally.

Adult texts were found to sow similar bitter seeds. The *Dictionnaire Apologétique de la Foi Catholique* (printed with Ecclesiastical approbation) records that Freemasons and Jews form a natural union as a climax "of the ancient pretensions and hatreds of the deicide people." Dom Prosper Gueranger's *Guide to the Church Liturgy* (most recently published with an Imprimatur in America in 1949) states: "The very sight of the chastisement inflicted on the murderers proclaims to the world that they [the Jews] were deicides. Their crime was an unparalleled one; its punishment is to be so too; it is to last to the end of time. . . . Cain-like, they shall wander, fugitives on the earth."

Churchmen and scholars are currently revising these texts and correcting the errors and biases contained in them.

Naturally, Jews must follow the same procedure of self-scrutiny and prejudice-purging in line with the sound injunction of Talmudic literature: "Cleanse thyself—then cleanse others!"

What position ought Jews to adopt on the question of dialogue? Should Jews accept the invitation of Pope Paul VI and others in Catholic and Protestant circles for "fraternal dialogue" and "trusting relations" in a happy future?

Opinions in Jewish circles have been sharply divided.

One group (generally found in Orthodox circles) rejects the concept of dialogue or ecumenism. The reasons may vary, but wary cynicism is common to all. Rabbi Joseph B. Soloveitchik writes that "there cannot be mutual understanding" between Jews and Christians on questions of doctrine and ritual or dogmas of our respective faiths because "Jews and Christians will employ different categories when touching matters like God, the Messiah, Jesus, Covenant, and Jewish law." On the other hand, Rabbi Soloveitchik declares that "when we move from the private world of faith to the public world of humanitarian and cultural endeavor, communication among the various faith communities is desirable and even essential." Others, such as Professor Eliezer Berkovits, Dr. Steven S. Schwarzschild, the Lubavitcher Rebbe, and Dr. Trude Weiss-Rosmarin, want no part of dialogue at all. They aver that anti-Semitism is a Christian problem—let Christians handle it. They fear dialogue as a possible step toward assimilation and baptism. They identify dialogue with the forced disputations of the Middle Ages, when Jews were compelled to defend their faith. In short, this group wants "neither the honey nor the sting" of ecumenism.

A second group believes dialogue imperative at all costs. They are not beyond flunkyism and *shtadlanut.* They spend fortunes on surveys and studies; they endow chairs at Christian universities and seminaries; they shuttle between New York and Rome; they adopt an often undignified posture. Their belief is that no price is too high to pay for interreligious peace and an end to anti-Semitism.

A third group maintains that dialogue is valuable, even essential. As Professor Abraham J. Heschel puts it: "To refuse contact with Christian theologians is to my mind barbarous." But they do not seek peace at any price and they insist that Jews must be treated as equals, as fellow children of God.

I believe that dialogue is possible and is vital. We must learn to live together in an ever-shrinking globe. We must join hands in confronting atheistic Communism. And we must in concert extirpate the religious roots of bias once and for all! To say that anti-Semitism is a Christian problem is to say that the victim of a crime should not seek redress from the criminal since it is the criminal's concern. Surely anti-Semitism is our problem as well; it impinges on our lives as Jews. We must do all in our power to fight it—provided we do so with dignity and self-respect.

If we are to learn from one another, if we are to live in amity, if we are to jointly stamp out the disease of religious hatred, then we must establish guideposts or norms for ecumenical dialogue.

What might those guideposts be?

Naturally, the first step must be the reevaluation of theological teachings about other faiths and the revision of sermons, prayers, and texts along the lines I have suggested. The teaching of contempt must end.

Secondly, we must approach each other with mutual respect, trust, and love. Pejoratives must be banished; superiority complexes must be eliminated. No faith can present itself as the "one true church" or the "*primus inter pares*" and expect there to be dialogue. Dialogue must not deteriorate into monologue; we must speak *to*—not *at*—one another.

Third, missionizing and proselytizing must be ruled out. Jews cannot join in harmony with Catholics who seek their union in the bosom of the Church, or with Lutherans who announce that "conversion of Jews is a matter of Christian conscience and commitment" (a resolution adopted at the Lutheran Convention of 1960). Ours is a world in which peaceful coexistence is an absolute necessity in the religious as well as in the political area. There is little difference between Khrushchev's brand of aggression, which proclaims that Communism will ultimately "bury" us, and a religious imperialism that takes the same position in regard to infidels and heretics. It is a short step from verbal imperialism to Crusades, Inquisitions, *Jihads* and religious wars. Consequently, if Christians and Jews are to live and work together they must accept Reinhold Niebuhr's view that it is "wrong and futile to attempt to convert Jews" for "Jews can find God more easily in terms of their own religious heritage." No religion has a monopoly on truth; none of us have all the keys to the kingdom. In the words of Micah (4:5): "For let all the nations walk in the name of their gods, while we will walk in the name of the Lord our God for ever and ever." The Talmud came to this conclusion seventeen centuries ago: "The righteous of all nations have a share in the World to Come."

Fourth, Christians must normalize their relationship to Jews and cease treating Judaism like a fossil, an ossified relic of a once-great faith, a legalistic, obsolete antiquity. I do not take kindly to being told that I am the "former Chosen People" whose Bible is an "Old Testament" and whose development was stunted nineteen centuries ago. Much could be accomplished in this area if Christians began to make their peace with the State of Israel. To be sure, the rebirth of the State caused a theological trauma in the minds of Protestants and Catholics. Both had taught that the loss of our Homeland came as punishment for rejecting Jesus; both had preached that only after Jews would accept baptism would they return to the Holy Land and witness the Second Coming of Christ. Pope Pius X made this clear to Theodor Herzl at their interview of January 25, 1904, when he announced that he could only support the Zionist cause if Jews would agree to be baptized. And when Pope Paul VI made his historic pilgrimage to Israel in January, 1964, he never once referred to the State by name and he entered via an obscure route at Megiddo. The Vatican still does not maintain diplomatic relations with Israel. It is as if the Church refuses to recognize this "fossil" as alive. But alive it is!

Finally, there is the danger that in our zeal to enter into interreligious dialogue with one another, we will present a distorted or incorrect image of our faith. The ill-informed layman who knows all about Christianity but little about Judaism could hardly be expected to represent Jewish theological norms with any authenticity. An "Ecumaniac" has been defined as "a person who knows all about other religions, but little about his own." It would be calamitous if semi-literate Jewish laymen whose knowledge of Torah was confined to redimentary Hebrew and Talmud Torah theology were our representatives at interreligious meetings. All that could result from such encounters would be misunderstanding, misrepresentation, and misinformation on all sides.

Unfortunately, such encounters are likely to increase as various agencies climb on the bandwagon of dialogue. One secular national Jewish organization has published a "kit" for "grass root," interreligious dialogue. I shudder as I contemplate zealous laymen, kit in hand, eagerly scurrying to represent Judaism at such a conference, barely capable of reading the prayers and quite prepared to "compromise" Jewish principles for the sake of good will. But as Professor Harry A. Wolfson of Harvard puts it, "Brotherhood implies the burying of the *hatchet*—not the burying of *convictions.*"

By all means let competent theologians join together in the mutual search for truth, justice, love, and peace; but let the uninformed, albeit well-intentioned layman keep hands off.

These, then, are the norms for fraternal dialogue.

The religious groups of the world have so much in common and such enormous need for dialogue. Their enemies are common enemies—atheism, materialism, Communism, Fascism, warfare, poverty, bigotry, ignorance. And their goals and Messianic dreams are shared in common as well—justice, brotherhood, love, and peace. Is it not time that we joined hands and walked together in harmony and mutual trust for the glory of God and man? Isaiah called upon us: "Come, let us reason together" (1:18). And the Psalmist sang: "Behold how good and pleasant it is for brethren to dwell together." [3]

Can we not bury past hates and reason together and dwell together in peace?

NOTES

[1] Romans 9:4-5
[2] Zephaniah 3:9

[3] Psalms 133:1

X

Race Relations

"Have we not one Father?
Has not one God created us?"

MALACHI 2:10

THE number *one* domestic problem in the United States
today is the problem of racial discrimination. It affects millions of American citizens—the American Indian, the Mex-
ican-American, the Puerto Rican—but most of all it affects
the 20 million American Negroes. The blackest stain on the
escutcheons of our nation is, doubtlessly, its treatment of
the blacks. And the origins of that shameful record go back
to the genesis of America.

For over two centuries the Negro suffered the anguish
and degradation of slavery. He had no family life, no security, no physical or mental safety, no peace of mind, no
hope. The government—local, state, and federal—was his
enemy. The judicial system was arrayed against him. Thus,
the Dred Scott Decision of 1857 considered him a mere
chattel, not a "man" in the eyes of the Constitution. And
the Plessy versus Ferguson Case (1896) described the
Negro as socially inferior to the white, hence destined to
segregation in "separate but equal" facilities.

Although President Abraham Lincoln had freed the slaves in his Emancipation Proclamation of 1863, his utterance was more proclamation than genuine emancipation. The Negro had a long, hard row to hoe; he was by no means a free and equal member of society.

In 1954, the historic Brown versus the Board of Education Decision struck down the notion of "separate but equal" schools. It was the turning point in Negro history in our country, the greatest moment since the Emancipation Proclamation. Segregation was about to gasp its last breath; a new era for the Negro was about to commence—or so it appeared at the time.

The enthusiasm, however, was premature: America's black community still has a long, painful road to travel. This is apparent from a cursory survey of the status of the Negro in America today, in the last years of the 1960's. The forces of state and local governments still are arrayed against the Negro in sections of the nation. Prejudices die slowly; fear and hatred linger like a winter night. And man's heart is often obdurate and venomous.

How goes it with the Negro today, a century after the Emancipation Proclamation?

Not well, I fear.

The American Negro is not benefitting from the enormous advances in medicine made in our land. His life expectancy is five years less than the average white; his infant mortality rate is 40 per cent higher. The Negro has poor and overcrowded hospitals; his prenatal and postnatal care are inferior to that of white families. Some white hospitals in the South have for a long time refused to treat Negro patients, thereby, in certain cases, causing the death of those patients. I myself have seen postnatal diseases neglected by Negro families because of the lack of adequate medical facilities, and with tragic results.

Emotional and mental illnesses also take their toll of the American Negro. Twice as many Harlemites as other groups are admitted to New York State mental hospitals yearly. The Negro has, after all, been made to feel inferior for so long that he often believes it himself. An old Negro proverb goes: "If you're white, you're right . . . if you're black, stay back." Having been nurtured on a diet of self-deprecation and little sense of personal worth and dignity, the Negro has lost faith in himself. "The worst crime the white man has committed has been to teach us to hate ourselves," said the late Malcolm X. The high rate of mental illness among Negroes reflects the emotional atmosphere in which the Negro has grown.

Nor has the American Negro kept up with his white neighbor in enjoying the economic blessings of the richest land on earth. The income of the average white family in 1967 was $7,717; the average Negro family earned $3,971. Sixty per cent of America's Negroes earn less than $3,000 —the so-called "poverty level" determined by the government. In Mississippi, Negro families are actually *starving* in this affluent land of plenty. While the national unemployment level hovers around the 4 per cent mark, the Negro rate is twice that total—about 650,000, or 20 per cent of the unemployed in America. In some slum areas, as many as 25 per cent of the Negroes are unemployed. Undoubtedly, automation hurts the Negro more than the white. He has had less education and training in skilled jobs, and his unskilled work is readily taken over by machines.

The craft unions have been the worst offenders in discriminating against the Negro. In Baltimore, for example, there were no Negro apprentices among steamfitters, sheet-metal workers or plumbers in 1967. The same situation obtains in Pittsburgh, Washington, and elsewhere. There is not one Negro and only one Puerto Rican leader in the International Ladies Garment Workers Union.

American Negroes have achieved dramatic break-throughs in civil service and government posts, but not in the private sectors of American economy. Many deliberately enter the armed services where they now can make significant advances, but they still cannot break through in many sectors of business, labor, and industry. Job discrimination is still the norm.

Consequently, the economic progress of the black community lags desperately. Thousands of Negroes have been forced on the relief rolls as congenital recipients of welfare assistance. One third of the nation's public aid goes to the Negro, although the Negro constitutes but 11 per cent of the population. In Chicago, one fourth of the Negroes are on relief and the same situation exists in New York, Philadelphia, Los Angeles, and elsewhere. President Lyndon B. Johnson estimated in his "Civil Rights Message to Congress" (February 15, 1967) that the gross national product would rise 30 billion dollars if discrimination ended.

America's Negroes lag in education as well. The United States Civil Rights Commission reported to President Johnson on February 20, 1967, that the disparity between the white and Negro educational levels is marked. The average Negro has 3 years less education than the average white; 20.3 per cent of the colored high school students drop out as compared to 8.5 per cent of the whites. The Negro schools are old and dilapidated; their classes are over-crowded; their teachers and courses inferior; their libraries are inadequate; their institutions generally stigmatized. The Commission noted that while there is no innate mental inferiority among colored students, they do not achieve as well as whites. Few enter colleges; 67.5 per cent failed the armed force's pre-induction mental test (as opposed to 18.8 per cent of whites), and the 1960 census showed that 20 per cent of the Negroes over age twenty-five were functionally illiterate!

The Brown versus the Board of Education Decision has, happily, given impetus to change in the education picture. Schools up North are integrated, although *de facto* segregation based on neighborhood ghettos does still exist. Down South, integration is still but a token in intransigent areas like Alabama, Mississippi, and Louisiana. There has been little speed and much deliberateness in implementing that historic Court decision.

But there are encouraging signs. Colleges are open to Negroes with poorer past records than whites. Even Ivy League schools are recruiting qualified Negroes. The Negro college graduate, who formerly earned less than a white high school graduate, is beginning to make his mark in white-collar trades and big firms. Bussing of students up North has broken down *de facto* segregation—often to the dismay of reluctant whites. Much is yet to be accomplished if the Negro is to reach the educational level of the white, and integration seems to be the key. The Civil Rights Commission surmised that Negro achievement would rise as much as *two grades* if Negro children would associate with classmates from better backgrounds and home environments.

Political discrimination also crushes the Negro. Long disenfranchised in the Southern states, many colored folk are too intimidated to vote even today. There has been dramatic progress, however. The number of black voters was up from 1,238,000 to over 2,700,000 in ten years. But only 50 per cent of Negroes take the trouble to vote up North!

The Negro office holder is entering the limelight. In 1954 there but two Negro congressmen; by 1967 there were seven, including a Senator from Massachusetts. Negro judges sit on the highest benches; Negro cabinet members assist the President; Negro mayors lead American cities.

Yet, many areas of political life resist change. Southern juries invariably exclude colored members. And the Negro has not achieved political power commensurate with his numbers even up North—not to mention the South.

The one area that shows the least progress for America's Negroes is the area of social relations. In social matters, prejudices manifest themselves most virulently and stubbornly. A bigot may not be too ruffled about a Negro voter, but he may explode at the thought of a Negro neighbor or golf partner.

In the matter of housing, for example, social prejudice has hurt the Negro, and hurt him badly. Despite open-housing laws in seventeen states and forty cities, the Negro still lives, on the whole, in overcrowded, dilapidated, rat-infested slums up North, or disreputable shanties down South.

Negro housing is overcrowded. In Harlem, 267,000 people are packed like sardines in a three-and-a-half square-mile area with a density of 105 people per acre. Half the buildings were built in the nineteenth century. In Los Angeles' Watts section, 32.5 per cent of the dwellings are overcrowded as compared to the national average of 11.5 per cent.

The dwellings are usually unsafe, unsanitary and unwholesome. Only 56 per cent of Negro dwellings in America meet normal health and safety standards. Rats and vermin share the quarters; cold water and no heat turn bleak hovels into refrigerators in the winter; poor ventilation makes incinerators out of them in summer.

Even when the Negro has a good job, an adequate salary, and a professional degree, he finds it nearly impossible to climb out of the black ghetto. Whites won't sell to him. Whites won't rent to him. Whites won't live next to him. A survey of 45 Negro professionals who moved into an upper-New York State city showed the frustration. After one year, only 22 had decent housing; 8 left the community in disgust. As President Johnson dourly observed, "The bullets at the battlefield do not discriminate, but the landlords at home do."

It goes without saying that social discrimination affects the Negro in his recreational facilities. Beach clubs, golf clubs, resorts, hotels, and restaurants remain off limits. Even the Negro serviceman finds that while his life is acceptable on the battlefield, his presence is scorned on a ball field.

Thus, the American Negro has been lynched and assaulted, brutalized and terrorized, discriminated against and humiliated, excluded and scorned. The state has been his enemy; the police his nemesis; the white man his oppressor. Stranger in his own land, pariah in his own house, the American Negro has suffered—and reflected that suffering —in predictable fashion.

The Negro family and society are demoralized. The family structure, already shattered by the slave system, has been further undermined by the patterns of prejudice.

Negro families, notes Whitney Young, have no consistent breadwinner. Consequently, the father has lost his role, and the matriarchy seems to prevail in Negro homes. The Negro male has been emasculated by the white society; he commands no respect, no position of honor, no steady employment. His wife often earns more than he does. Small wonder, then, that one-fifth of Harlem males are separated from the wives (the New York average is one of thirty) while two of seven Negro women are separated (the New York average is one of sixteen). Only 50 per cent of Harlem children have both parents; the New York City average is 83 per cent.

There are other disasterous side effects: The Negro crime rate is appallingly high. The Harlem juvenile delinquency rate is twice the New York City level. There are ten times the number of drug addicts in Harlem as in the rest of the City of New York. Alcoholism corrodes Negro society.

A further trauma of the plight of the Negro is his loss of self-esteem, personal worth, and individual dignity. Call a man an animal long enough and he begins to act like one; brand a human a sub-human, and he plays the role. Having stripped the Negro of his identity, his worth, his self respect, white America cannot expect the Negro to pull himself up by his bootstraps overnight.

The Negro is not fully capable of self-help. Even the Negro millionaires (and there are surprisingly many) have, until recently, scorned their pathetic brethren. But the average Negro whose dreams have shrivelled like "a raisin in the sun" (to borrow the poignant phrase of Langston Hughes) cannot climb out of the abyss, cannot make it on his own. He has little initiative and he has the omnipresent welfare cycle on which to rely. Why should he climb out only to be clubbed down again by a hostile white world?

A final—and frighteningly new—result of America's shameful treatment of its Negro minority is the development of violence in the black community. Violence, after all, ultimately engenders violence; hatred breeds more hatred. Pent-up frustrations must sooner or later spill over like the lava of a great volcano. Bombings of churches, lynchings of helpless Negro farmers, murder of civil-rights workers, clubbing of women demonstrators, fire-hosing of peaceful pickets, dog attacks on nonviolent protestors—all were destined to evoke an eruption. And they did.

It came with hurricane fury and venom in Harlem, Watts, Newark, Cleveland, Philadelphia, Atlanta, Chicago, Rochester, and Detroit. Negroes looted, injured, killed, smashed, and burned in an orgy of hate than was unseen for a century in this land.

New extremist groups began to crop up. The Black Muslims gained new adherents to their policy of hatred for the "white devil" and rejection of integration as a farce and a white stratagem. Other black nationalists called for "Black Power." "Black Power" implies financial and political power for the Negro—a worthy goal. But it also connotes violence, hate, mayhem, and even murder.

Suddenly hates long suppressed, long denied, burst forth. Hate the white! Hate the state! Hate the police! Hate the Jew!

Yes, even the Jew was singled out as a scapegoat for the frustrations of the Negro. The Jew who had struggled with adversity and fought against prejudice; the Jew who had come up from the sweatshop and scrambled out of the tenament was now, pathetically, singled out by some Negro leaders and their numerous followers as the enemy.

True, some Jews are slumlords. And some are exploiters. And some are bigoted. But Jews created the Negro College Fund and the National Association for the Advancement of Colored People, and Jews financed and manned the civil-rights battles North and South in disproportionate numbers.

Some Negroes have forgotten these facts. Why should they remember? Now *they* are prejudiced; *they* are blinded to truth; *they* suffer from reversed racism. And a prejudiced person is incapable of seeing the truth and judging persons, as the martyred Dr. Martin Luther King Jr. put it so beautifully, "no longer by the color of their skin but by the content of their character."

Moderates like Roy Wilkins, A. Philip Randolph, Whitney Young, and Bayard Rustin are going to be hard pressed to contain the radicals and avert explosions and violence in the days ahead. Professor Kenneth B. Clark warns: "As long as this chasm between white and dark America is allowed to exist, racial tensions and conflicts, hatred and fear will spread." James Baldwin, the brilliant and acerbic Negro novelist, writes in *The Fire Next Time* that the Negro no longer believes in the good faith of white Americans. He describes the Negro plight in these bitter words:

> *You were born where you were born and faced the future that you faced because you were black and* for no other reason. *The limits of your ambition were, thus, expected to be set forever. You were born into a society which spelled out with brutal clarity, and in as*

> *many ways as possible, that you were not expected to*
> *aspire to excellence: you were expected to make*
> *peace with mediocrity.*

Baldwin ends on an ominous note as he quotes the Negro folksong: "God gave Noah the rainbow sign, no more water, the fire next time!"

We face the real possibility that "burn baby, burn"—the fearful slogan of Watts—will become the byword of desperate Negroes throughout the land. The Negro is in revolt, as Louis Lomax notes, and unless white America joins him in the vanguard, that revolt will become a nightmare and a bloodbath. Either we must prepare for greater racial violence, or we must all support a peaceful Negro revolution.

Above all, I am convinced, religion must not sit by (as it has often done in the past) silently detached, preoccupied with other-worldly matters. It must lead, not follow. Discrimination and prejudice are the antitheses of religion: religion (at least the Jewish religion) teaches love and justice for all men. Judaism offers many rich insights in the realm of human relations and it merits man's attention. It is to this theme that I now turn.

Unquestionably, the greatest teaching Judaism has offered to humanity, along with its idea of monotheism, is its concept of the Divine origin and brotherhood of man. "God created man in His image," records the Book of Genesis (1:26; 5:1f; 9:5f.). Divine breath fills his soul; God's hand is manifest in his body. Each man, therefore, bears the stamp of his Maker; each human being shelters a spark of the Lord. He is but "a little lower than the angels" (Psalms 8:5ff.).

"Precious is man," observed Rabbi Akivah, "because he is created in God's image." [1] Significantly Rabbi Akivah uses the Hebrew noun *adam*—one of the generic terms for "mankind," "humanity." As a result, man's body and soul must be revered and cared for. Hillel was once asked by a student why he was rushing so. He answered: "I am rushing to perform a religious duty." "What duty are you going to perform?" asked the student. "The duty of taking a bath," he replied. "Do not the pagans wash and scrub the images and statues of their deities? Shall I not, accordingly, wash my body which was created in God's image?" [2] Man's body and mind are creations of God; they must be accorded proper respect.

Man is God's child. It follows, therefore, that all men are brothers. "Have we not one Father? Has not one God created us? Why then do men deal treacherously with each other?" [3] It is noteworthy that all the creatures fashioned by God were subdivided into species; [4] man alone among the creatures was created in *one* species. [5]

Mankind is united by virtue of its common ancestor. This is evidently the point of the Adam and Eve saga; it is also the intention of the tenth chapter of Genesis, which lists all of the nations and tribes of the world as having descended from *one common father*, namely, Adam, and his postdiluvian descendant Noah.

That archetypal Adam, the forefather of us all, was depicted by the sages as a composite of all men, all races, and all nations. Rabbi Meir taught that Adam was composed of dust from all parts of the world, and another view held that the members of his body came from all nations of the world. [6] A remarkable legend records that the first man consisted of different colored clay—red, black, white, and green—thus reminding us that all races descend from one progenitor.[7] "All men are shaped from the same mold as Adam," notes a Talmudic rabbi, "and yet no man resembles his neighbor." [8]

A number of significant concepts flow from the notions that man is created in God's image, that all men are God's children, and that all are brothers. The first principle is the supreme worth of every single individual, of each and every being. Each man is described by ancient and medieval sages as a microcosm of the world, a universe in miniature. Consequently, when one destroys or injures or shames a fellow creature, it is as if an entire world had suffered.[9] The supreme worth of the individual is reflected in Jewish law and ethics, in theology and homily. Professor Moshe Greenberg notes that life and property were commensurable in ancient pagan and Bedouin law, but this is never the case in the Bible, where man is not an instrument or means, but an end; where the value of a single life is all supreme. The most striking passage in this regard is the following:

> *Therefore Adam was created singly to teach us that whoever destroys a single life is considered by the Bible as if he had destroyed an entire world. And whoever saves a single life is considered by the Bible to have saved an entire world. In addition, no person may destroy the peace of humanity by saying, "My forefather was greater than yours". . . . Therefore every individual is obliged to declare, "The world was created for my sake."* [10]

Murder is a heinous offense, for human life is sacred. Cain's murder of Abel is recorded for all of history to note, and the Ten Commandments [11] list murder as a cardinal sin. Whosoever sheds the blood of a man created in God's image forfeits his own life, for he has "diminished God's image." [12]

Life must be preserved at all cost. If one sees a person in danger of drowning, of being torn by a wild beast, or of being assaulted by brigands, one is duty bound to try to save the victim.[13] If one fails to do so, he has violated the Biblical command, "You shall not stand on the blood of your brother."

Nor may one "set aside one life in order to save another, even one's own." If a ruler orders you to kill so-and-so, or else forfeit your own life, you must forfeit your own life, for who says that your blood is redder than the other's? [14] If an enemy troop has besieged a city and demands that a woman be delivered for defilement, all should submit to defilement rather than betray the one.[15] The Tosefta rules that a besieged town may *not* deliver up a hostage to the enemy for execution even if all are thereby imperiled.[16] If the enemy specified a certain person, and if—as Professor Saul Lieberman interprets the passage—the man is guilty of a crime and liable to be executed, then and only then may the populace turn him over.

In short, bloodshed pollutes the earth we walk on, and murder diminishes God's presence in the world, for every human being is, in part, sacred, and every life is precious. The conclusion of Jewish law reflects this view with clarity and definitiveness: "Under threat of death, a Jew may break all the commandments of the Torah save three—one may not indulge in idolatry, sexual immorality, or murder." [17]

The notion of human freedom is also connected with the

Jewish ideal of the value of the human being. Israel (first among the peoples of the earth) has always been intoxicated with the notion of freedom. We were born in the crucible of Egyptian slavery: we could still feel the taskmaster's lash, still taste the bread of affliction, and we still recall the anguish of the slaying of our male children.

Consequently, our central festival became Passover—"the season of freedom." We proclaimed liberty throughout the land and to all its inhabitants (Leviticus 25:10). We sought to humanize, if not abolish, the institution of slavery, for man is God's servant, not man's. Thus, a Hebrew slave went free every seventh and fiftieth year. No one had the right to prevent his legal emancipation.[18] If he chose slavery over freedom he was to be humiliated and mutilated—disgraced publicly for having opted for slavery. He was to be given fair treatment, decent food and lodging, freedom to practice religious rites. He was never to be beaten or mutilated; killing a Hebrew slave was a capital crime. "He who purchases a Hebrew slave purchases a master over himself," noted the Talmud.[19] As Professor Boaz Cohen has demonstrated, Hebrew slavery really became a benevolent form of "civil bondage"—and long before the Romans advanced to that point of human progress.

Pagan slaves were likewise treated decently. They went free if abused or manhandled. They were not mere animals or "animated tools" (Aristotle's phrase). In fact, Rabban Gamaliel and Rabbi Jose mourned the death of their decent and righteous slaves as if they had lost relatives.[20] Later Jewish law required the master to convert pagan slaves to Judaism and free them entirely. In the eyes of God, "rich and poor meet, for the Lord has made them all." [21] And as Job so nobly affirmed in his "confession of innocence"

"Have I despised the cause of my manservant or of my maidservant? . . . Did not He make him in the womb as He made me and fashion us both alike in the womb?" [22]

Freedom for all men of all economic classes and strata is the inescapable logic of Judaism's concept of man.

Another ineluctable concept that flows from the notion of the Divine origin of man and human brotherhood is the imperative to *love* one's fellow creature. The Golden Rule of Judaism is Leviticus 19:18: "Love your neighbor as yourself." Rabbi Akivah viewed this as the great and most comprehensive rule of Judaism.[23] On the other hand, Ben Azzai considered the verse in Genesis 5:1 as even more inclusive and fundamental: "This is the book of the generation of Adam, on the day God created Adam in the image of God he created him." Ben Azzai sought to demonstrate that we cannot love our fellowman until we realize our common origin, the Divine in every man, and the fundamental brotherhood of the human race.

Hillel, too, stressed the notion of love for all creatures as basic to Judaism. When approached by a would-be convert and asked for the essence of the Faith, he replied: "That which is hateful to you, do not do to your friend. This is the essence of the Torah; the rest is mere commentary. Now go and study the rest!" [24]

Whether love of neighbor applies to gentile as well as Jew has been debated for centuries. The context of the Golden Rule in Leviticus 19:18 is not clear in this regard. Some of the sages whose attitude towards the pagan world (not to mention the Christian and Moslem world) was embittered by gentile persecutions of the Jewish People, did not include gentiles in the commandment to love one's neighbor. Their particularism reflected personal suffering.

On the other hand, there is abundant evidence that the Jew is expected to love *all* men, irrespective of religion or national origin. Thirty-six times does the Bible command us to love the stranger and foreigner, for we Jews were once strangers and foreigners in the Land of Egypt. Some of the greatest sages in Israel urged us to love all men, even those who were crushing and oppressing us. Hillel exhorted us to love *all* "creatures" (*beriyot* in Hebrew is another generic term for "creatures," "humanity") and to bring them close to Torah.[25] Rabbi Joshua (who lived after the destruction of the Second Temple when anti-Roman feelings were most bitter) cautioned that "hatred of humanity destroys a person." [26] Rabban Yohanan ben Zaccai, who actually witnessed the calamity, boasted that he always was first to greet his fellowman with the blessing of peace—including gentiles in the market place.[27] And Abaya, during the third century, in Babylonia, exhorted Jews to "spread peace among their brethren, kinsmen, and all men—even gentiles in the market place, so that all may be acceptable to God on high and beloved of man below." [28]

It is remarkable that in view of the fearful suffering Jews endured at the hands of the pagan Romans and medieval Christians and Moslems, Jewish tradition did not, on the whole, succumb to bigotry and unmitigated chauvinism. The Talmud had ruled that the righteous gentiles have a portion in the age to come; that virtue is not a racial or inherited trait, but is within the grasp of all men who must be judged on their own merits.[29] In numerous legal discussions, the Talmud (and the code books as well) stresses that we must deal "peaceably" with our gentile neighbor: We must return his lost property; we must not defraud or cheat him, steal from him or injure him; and we must give him charity, visit his sick, and bury his dead.[30] In the middle ages, when Christian-Jewish relations were at their worst, when Crusades ravaged Jewish communities, and the Church humiliated and degraded us, legalists and preachers still insisted that Jews must deal honestly and ethically with *all* men. As Rabbi Moses of Coucy wrote: "Jews must conduct themselves with Jew and gentile truthfully . . . lest the gentiles say, 'See, this is the People whom God chose; they are all thieves and knaves.'" The authorities agree that it is a *worse* sin to cheat a gentile because by doing so the Jew profanes God's name and besmirches the reputation of the Torah and the Jewish People (*hillul ha-Shem*).

Because the Jew is to consider all men as brothers and deal lovingly toward them, he is commanded to safeguard the dignity and honor of all creatures. To borrow Martin Buber's formulation, we must relate to our neighbor as an "I" to a "thou," not as an "I" to an "it," for our neighbor is not a thing: he is God's child.

One of the most remarkable concepts in Jewish law and theology is the notion of *kevod ha-beriyot*—literally, "the honor of mankind" or "human dignity." The concept of *kevod ha-beriyot* in Jewish sources is, in the words of Dr. Max Kadushin, an illustration of an ethical value-concept overriding other *mitzvot*.

Indeed, the sages rule that human dignity overrides *all* rabbinic ordinances; some go so far as to say it negates Biblical law as well. There are several aspects to this remarkable concept. First a Jew may perform a prohibited act for the sake of human dignity; second, a Jew may abstain from performing a positive commandment for the same reason; finally, every Jew must treat all people with reverential regard for their honor and dignity. There are a number of illustrations of this amazingly sensitive concept scattered throughout rabbinic literature.[31]

The notion of "human dignity" and the "honor of mankind" extends to all of God's creatures. This is evidently the reason for the use of the generic term *beriyot*, which implies all men, all races, and all religions. Gentiles are also subsumed under this category, as is indicated in a midrashic story of how Rabbi Eleazar ben Shamua rescued, fed, and clothed a Roman survivor of a shipwreck. Later, the Roman was elected emperor; he returned the favor to Rabbi Eleazar because the sage had been wise and magnanimous in safeguarding human dignity.[32]

The notion of *kevod ha-beriyot* is sensitively constructed; it seeks to consider the most intimate feelings of a human being. "The Omnipresent has concern for human dignity," declare the Rabbis. "His law provides that a man who wants to be excused from the army because he has built a new house or betrothed a girl must bring proof. But not the fainthearted or cowardly: he need not impair his honor by bringing proof." [33]

Even criminals have dignity, for they, too, are God's children. Rabban Yohanan ben Zaccai noted that a thief who has stolen an ox pays five-fold restitution, while a thief who has stolen a lamb pays only four-fold. Why the difference? Because, says Rabban Yohanan, the thief merely led the ox by the muzzle, while the sheep-thief carried the lamb on his shoulders and thus impaired his dignity. Consequently, the sheep-thief pays a lesser fine.[34] Several other remarkably sensitive laws show rabbinic solicitude for the honor of mankind in ways we would not expect. Thus, God closed the mouth of Balaam's talking ass lest it tell of

Balaam's folly. So, too, animals used for zoophilia were ordered killed lest they add to the degradation of the sinners by their presence. And God's concern for human dignity is seen, we are told, in the law requiring the destruction of "high places" used for idolatry so that those symbols of human depravity would not be preserved to commemorate the sin.[35]

Human feelings must be considered in all the day-to-day dealings between man and man. Verbal insults and abuse are not tolerated; the later *halakhah* provides monetary fines and flogging for persons who slandered their neighbor.[36] Medieval authorities like Asher ben Yehiel of Spain, Meir of Rothenberg from Germany, the Italian Talmudist Joseph Colon, and the Polish Moses Isserles were terribly strict in applying the laws against humiliating a child of God. The following statements illustrate the point with clarity:

The person who slanders his fellowman never can be forgiven.[37]

Rabbi Akivah says: "Even the poorest Israelite is to be considered like a freeman down on his luck, for they are all sons of Abraham, Isaac, and Jacob. Hence, if one insults a fellow, one must pay all equally."[38]

He who impairs the dignity of his fellow, impairs the dignity of the Omnipresent, for man was created in the image of God.[39]

Rabbi Jose ben Haninah taught: "He who derives honor by shaming his fellowman loses his portion in the age to come."[40]

He who humiliates his fellowman in public it is as if he had murdered him.[41]

I can think of no better text to sum up the insistence of Judaism on protecting human dignity than this:

The stones of the altar have no sense of right or wrong. Yet God said that you should not treat them disrespectfully. A fortiori, it is logical that you must refrain from treating with disrespect your fellowman who is made in the image of Him by whose word the world came into being.[42]

Does the obligation to preserve and safeguard human dignity apply to all *races?* Is the Bible color-blind? Or does it in fact condone racialism and recognize the superiority of racial or ethnic groups?

Segregationists claim that the Bible is the basis for their viewpoint. Thus, they quote the story of Noah and his son Ham.[43] Ham had disgraced his father and mocked his drunken debauchery. In turn, Noah cursed Ham and his descendants, including the Ethiopians and the black races. This, we are told, proves that God cursed the colored people and ordained that they be slaves to whites.

Another favorite text for racialism is Numbers 12:1ff. There we read how Miriam and Aaron disparaged Moses for marrying a Cushite woman (that is, an Ethiopian Negress). Racists aver that the Bible frowned on miscegenation, and that the story of Moses proves the rectitude of their position.

Yet another ludicrous illustration of how the Devil can often quote (and misquote) Scripture for his own nefarious purpose is this: the Afrikaans version of the Bible, published in apartheid-ridden South Africa, refused to translate Song of Songs 1:5 as the Hebrew requires: "Black and comely am I." Why? The South African theologians opined: "No one can be *black* and comely." Hence, they translated the verse to read: "I am comely and burnt brown by the sun."

There are some who detect in the idea of the Chosen People a rationale for chauvinism and the racial superiority of Jews over other ethnic groups. Anti-Semites delight in pointing to the notion of the Chosen People as evidence that the Hebrews, and not the Nazis, introduced racial prejudice into Western civilization.

These charges are all, to be sure, canards. Any objective student who possesses a sound knowledge of Hebrew language and literature can readily expose the fraud. Undoubtedly some Jews in antiquity became intoxicated with the notion of the Chosen People and lauded it over their pagan neighbors. But to imply that Judaism introduced racial superiority into the Western world (as Arnold Toynbee writes) is an obscene distortion of fact. Surely some Jews were prejudiced against dark-skinned peoples, but to argue that these prejudices represent authentic, normative Judaism is to misrepresent Judaism.

The so-called curse against Ham and the Negro race is really a curse directed against Ham's descendant Canaan—Israel's sworn enemy. The Canaanites were *not* a colored race; they were as white as the Hebrews or Greeks. The racial exegesis of this passage in Genesis is faulty.

As to the matter of the wife of Moses, here too, a simple reading of the text would dispel the racial interpretation. The Bible clearly indicates God's displeasure with Miriam and Aaron.[44] In fact, He smites Miriam with leprosy, turning her skin "as white as snow," as if to teach us that white skin is not necessarily superior to dark: it can be a symptom of disease and death. Moreover, the nature of Aaron's and Miriam's charge against Moses is not clear at all. Some conclude that Moses was chided for having sinned by separating from Zipporah, his wife (who was actually a Midianite and not a Cushite). They translate the word "Cushite" to mean "beautiful," for Zipporah was as beautiful as a Cushite, both in body and character, and she deserved better treatment by Moses. On the other hand, there is a legend that Moses married a second wife—an Ethiopian queen. Aaron and Miriam criticized him for *bigamy*, not for interracial marriage.[45]

The South African view that "no one can be black and comely" is totally untenable and palpably false: the Hebrew *shechora* means "black" and not "sunburnt," as any Hebrew school child knows. Moreover, there is ample evidence in Hebrew sources that black-skinned people were *not* viewed with disdain. Unusual, yes; abhorrent, no. King Saul and his daughter Michal were allegedly dark-skinned and as beautiful as Ethiopians. The Queen of Sheba, one of Solomon's wives, was an Ethiopian who was dark, comely, and wise. And the rabbis of the Midrash frequently use the metaphor that one is as outstanding in good deeds as a Negro is outstanding because of his color. One of the noblest Negroes mentioned in the Bible was Eved Melech, the Ethiopian eunuch, who saved the life of the Prophet Jeremiah while risking his own life at the hands of the pro-Egyptian courtiers.[46] Later legends extol the courage and virtue of the Ethiopian hero.[47] A superb medieval Midrash depicts the Messianic era as one in which Ethiopian, Ger man, and Jew will walk hand in hand in comity and brotherhood.

No, there is absolutely no basis in Biblical or Rabbinic sources for treating colored people as inferiors. Any attempt to find scriptural basis for racialism and segregation is merely a ploy and a canard. "Behold you are just like the Ethiopians unto me," said the Lord to an overly puffed-up People of Israel.[48]

As to those who detect in the Jewish notion of the Chosen People the germ of racialism, one need merely turn to the Prophet Amos to understand that chosenness means *noblesse oblige*—duty, not privilege, higher standards, not haughty disdain. "Only you have I known from all the peoples of the earth; therefore I shall hold you more responsible for your iniquities."[49] Chosenness is always linked with service, with higher ethical standards, with the insuperable task of bearing God's message to an indifferent and hostile world. It implies, as the Second Isaiah put it, a sacred mission incumbent upon the Jew to be the Servant of the Lord—often reviled, often bruised and killed, but never harming others. And the sages coupled the chosenness ideal to the concept of Torah: Jews were chosen not because of superiority or might or numbers, but in order that they might teach Torah and ethics to the world and abide by God's *mitzvot*.

In sum, Judaism and racialism are utterly incompatible and irreconcilable. This is Judaism's appraisal of man, its outlook on the matter of race prejudice. It is, in my judgment, man's best hope for curing the ulcer of bigotry in an ever-shrinking world—provided we implement these ideals and incorporate them into daily living.

Albert Camus once observed that we humans are all condemned to live together in this world. This world consists of all kinds of people—of diverse nations, races, religions, and ideologies. Either we learn to live together as brothers, wrote Martin Luther King Jr., or we perish together as fools. There is no alternative. We either solve the Negro problem at home, or we face the probability of a racial explosion that will make Mount Etna look like a firecracker. We either join forces with moderates in advancing the cause of human rights, or we will witness the emergence of radicals and hate-mongers whose venom and violence will eclipse that of Malcolm X. We either end racialism abroad and in every land, or we must be prepared for wars between blacks and whites and yellows and browns that will dwarf the Crusades and the World Wars.

On the other hand, the colored peoples of the world much eschew racialism in reverse. Negro leaders must condemn anti-Semitism unequivocally. They must not tolerate anti-white agitation. Nor may they sit by silently and condone the appalling looting and rioting that have shattered and bloodied so many American cities. Lawlessness and mayhem are not the answers to the Negro plight. Nor can anyone excuse pillaging as the Negro's legitimate response to exploitation, prejudice, and police brutality. It would be tragic beyond belief if Negroes fell prey to the white man's disease of racialism.

We who have been witness to the decimation of six million kinsmen for no other reason than that they were Jews, appreciate only too well the malignancy of racialism. "No man is an island entire of itself; every man is a piece of the continent, a part of the main," wrote the English poet and theologian, John Donne. We are all part of the human story; our fates are inextricably intertwined. All men's suffering and degradations are ours too; sooner or later, all suffer for the sin of racialism. Yesterday the Jew; today the Negro; tomorrow—who knows?

Our Faith—predicated on the notion that God has created our forefather Adam in his image and that all men are descended from Adam; that all are brothers, and each is imbued with the Spark of Divinity—our Faith has formulated the ideal of human brotherhood for the world. Will the world accept it?

The poet Edward Markham once wrote:

The crest and crowning of all good,
Life's final star is Brotherhood;
Our hope is in heroic men,
Star-led to build the world again;
To this even the ages ran,
Make way for Brotherhood, make way for man!

With Judaism's program for brotherhood, heroic men can yet reach that final star and transmute the jungle into Paradise.

NOTES

1 Avot III, 14; Avot de Rabbi Nathan 39, p. 56
2 Genesis Rabbah XXXIV, 3
3 Malachi 2:10
4 Genesis 1:24f.
5 Genesis 1:26f.
6 Sanhedrin 38af.
7 Louis Ginzberg, *Legends of the Jews*, V, 72, n.15
8 Sanhedrin 37a
9 Avot de Rabbi Nathan 31, pp.

46af; cf. *Sefer Hassidim* 44, p. 103, ed. Margolioth
10 Mishnah Sanhedrin IV, 5; Gemara 37af. Avot de Rabbi Nathan 31, p. 45b
11 Exodus 20:13; Deuteronomy 5:17
12 Genesis 9:5f; Mekilta II, 262; Genesis Rabbah XXXIV, 14; Sanhedrin 58b
13 Sifra on Leviticus 19:16, p. 89a

14 Pesahim 25b
15 M. Terumah VIII, 12
16 Terumah VII, 20, ed. Lieberman pp. 148f.
17 Sanhedrin 7a; *passim*
18 Jeremiah 34:8 ff.
19 Kiddushin 29a
20 Mishnah and Gemara Berakhot 16b; Maimonides, *Code*, "Mourning," XII, 12
21 Proverbs 22:2
22 Job 31:15
23 Sifra *ad locum*, p. 89b; *passim*
24 Shabbat 21a; Yer. Nedarim IX, 4; 4c; Avot de Rabbi Nathan 15 and 16, pp. 29b ff.; Tobit 4:15, etc.
25 Avot I, 12
26 Avot II, 11
27 Berakhot 17a
28 *Ibid.*
29 Avodah Zarah 10b; Tosefta Sanhedrin XIII, 2; Sanhedrin 59a; Sifra on Leviticus 18:5, p. 86b; Seder Eliyahu, p. 48, ed. Friedman, etc.
30 Gittin 61a; Baba Kama 113b; Hulin 91a, 94a, etc.

31 cf. Berakhot 19; Yer. Berakhot III, 1; 6a, b; Baba Metzia 29bf; Shabbat 94b, and *passim*
32 Koheleth Rabbah XI, 1
33 Sifré Numbers § 192, p. 110a
34 Mekilta III, 99; Baba Kama 79b
35 Numbers Rabbah XX, 14; Sifra on Leviticus 20:15, p. 92b
36 Pesahim 113b; Kiddushin 28a
37 Yer. Baba Kama VIII, 10; 6c; Gemara 83a, 96a, 90af.
38 Mishnah B.K. VIII, 6; Gemara 83a, 86a, 90f.
39 Genesis Rabbah XXIV, 7; B.M. 58f; Sanhedrin 68b
40 Yer. Hagigah II, 1; 77c
41 Baba Metziah 58b
42 Mekilta II, 291f.
43 Genesis 9:25
44 Numbers 12:6-13
45 Louis Ginzberg, *Legends of the Jews*, V, 407, note 80 and VI, 90, note 488
46 Jeremiah 38:1-13
47 Ginzberg, *op. cit.*, IV, 318 ff, and VI, 412, note 66
48 Amos 9:7
49 Amos 3:2

XI

The New Morality

> "Now the inhabitants of Sodom were
> very wicked sinners against the Lord."
>
> GENESIS 13:13

A SINGLE issue of the daily press can contain a devastating commentary on the morals of our times. The following items appeared in an issue of the *New York Times* one day, several years ago:

> *A jewel robbery amounting to a million dollars was perpetrated by five bandits. The robbery was witnessed by 25 to 30 workmen at a nearby demolition site. Not one of them told the police: instead, they enjoyed a wild spree of looting and caching diamonds, emeralds, and other precious stones.*
>
> *The Forest Hills General Hospital (New York) closed down after seven of its directors (some of whom are physicians) were indicted for cheating Blue Cross of $92,000 by padding payrolls.*
>
> *The Exchange Buffet Cafeteria, founded in 1885, was forced to close because of bankruptcy. The cafe-*

*teria chain had always operated under an honor sys-
tem whereby patrons would select their food and tell
the cashier what they had eaten. A spokesman for the
corporation declared that the policy of trusting the
customers had finally destroyed the firm.*

These three disquieting items merely reinforced the ob-
servations of many clergymen and laymen who are disturbed by what they consider the breakdown of morality
and ethics in our time. Professor Mordecai M. Kaplan has
depicted our society as enjoying a "religious boom and a
moral bust." Dr. Alfred Kinsey's studies—followed by
other similar projects—have shown that the virus of immorality has infected the once sacred domain of the home.
Frank Gibney's highly readable *The Operators* was an eye-
opening analysis of the erosion of ethical values in the
world of business. And Fred J. Cook exposed a similar phenomenon in public life in his volume, *The Corrupted Land.*

Look Magazine conducted a three-month study of
"Morality U.S.A." and concluded that "Bigness, the Bomb,
and the Buck have destroyed our old morality." The conclusion of the authors of the study was: "We are heading
into danger. We are in the midst of a moral crisis—because
the great majority of Americans, who want to try to live
moral lives, no longer can be certain what is right and what
is wrong."

All strata of our society seem to have been tinged and
tainted. Scientists like the late J. Robert Oppenheimer talk
of the feeling of "sin" they now experience as a result of
the Atomic Bomb. Nuclear physicists who were members
of a congregation I once served—men who had helped create the Bomb—still feel remorse over what some consider

to have been an immoral act. And we have all witnessed the depraved and criminal acts of German physicians and scientists who debased their professions by committing bestial and unspeakable crimes.

Government officials are not above reproach, either. Not long ago a New York State Supreme Court Justice went to jail for bribery. Senator Thomas Dodd of Connecticut has been censured by his colleagues for using campaign funds for personal expenses. In private life, such a breach of ethics might have merited a jail sentence. Representative Adam Clayton Powell's expensive and unnecessary junkets on alleged fact-finding missions are wastes of public funds. His disgracefully overloaded payroll and retinue of salaried absentee assistants have outraged even his normally lenient colleagues. When I expressed my disgust with Mr. Powell's flimflam to one of his close friends and associates (who himself has since been discharged from a prominent public post due to financial misconduct) he heatedly retorted: "*All* the congressmen are doing the same thing. The only reason why you are so upset is because he is black!"

Whenever a candidate accepts a campaign contribution from some vested interest or power lobby, is there not implicit in that check an expectation that at a future date, in a crucial vote, that candidate will vote to support the interests of the lobby? Bribes, after all, are not always offered in a crass, unsophisticated fashion. How does the average public servant resolve this conflict of interest without sacrificing his ethical principles?

Businessmen are similarly hard pressed to mix morals and profits: the choice between big profits and ethical business practices is not always a clear-cut one. Nor does the corporate official find it easy to resolve the dilemma of how to pay high corporation taxes and still present fat dividends to investors. All kinds of deceptive devices are used to increase the volume of business. Deceptive packaging, trading stamps, false advertising, collusive price-fixing—all are designed to insure higher profits at the expense of gullible consumers. The most reputable firms have duped the public into throwing away billions of dollars. For example, Americans have spent $100 million dollars on *fake* reducing pills!

Incredibly, manufacturers sometimes market dangerous, even lethal products. We all remember with terror the Thalidomide tragedy that maimed unborn infants for life. One of the most despicable cases of criminal neglect occurred in Morocco in 1959. Ten thousand people were paralyzed, some permanently, through the consumption of adulterated cooking oil that some ghoulish sharpers sold to unsuspecting peasants.

Other business practices that are widely utilized are equally questionable. Kickbacks, Christmas gifts, bonuses, and various honoraria amount to five billion dollars annually. One notorious practitioner of this fine art of the shakedown was a clothing purchaser for Sears who adeptly amassed a quarter of a million dollars from manufacturers. He even assigned one client the task of taking his aged parents to dinner each night of the week!

The expense account is another aberration of today's business. This subtle technique of illegally-padded accounts costs the government from five to ten billion dollars of vitally needed tax revenues.

Some of my business friends defend these stratagems by arguing that "you've got to do these things if you want to stay in business." Joel Schencker, prominent businessman and Broadway producer, writes: "We live in a culture that rewards the man who corners the market—this is completely contrary to the principles laid down by our rabbis. . . . The best you can do is to live the most reasonably honest life you can and to hurt as few people as possible."

In summing up the "businessman's moral failure," Dr. Louis Finkelstein wrote a trenchant and oft-quoted article that appeared in the magazine *Fortune:* "If American businessmen are right in the way most of them now live, then all the wise men of the ages, all the prophets and saints were fools. If the saints were not fools, the businessmen must be . . . they can defeat a local competitor but may well be defeated by the competitor of us all, which is moral decay."

Unfortunately, the labor movement has not escaped the plague either. Lord Acton's axiom, "power corrupts; absolute power corrupts absolutely" also holds true in the ranks of labor. All-powerful union bosses have placed personal greed above workers' needs. The poor union member sees his leader riding in expensive limousines and frequently drawing higher salaries than United States Congressmen, while few benefits accrue to the rank-and-file. Sometimes union bosses are in league with criminal elements. The Mafia—that sinister society of cutthroats and pirates—has not only moved into legitimate businesses but into union affairs as well. The figures of Dave Beck and James Hoffa, rather than David Dubinsky and Walter Reuther, are, unfortunately, conjured up when we think of the typical "labor leader."

The erosion of ethical standards is likewise evident in our daily living. Every sector of our private lives reflects, I fear, the decline of morality typical of our times.

For example, our ideas on sex have changed radically; our culture is sex-obsessed. Our movies, plays, and novels are failures unless they deal with erotic themes. I have watched dejectedly the debasement of taste in the public media. Prurient scenes that were once taboo are now legal in movies; lewd language is *de rigueur* in books; television shows that depict sex with embarrassing frankness are now legitimate; and some critically acclaimed Broadway plays are actually obscene. A prominent movie executive decried this new trend in the entertainment media and lamented the loss of clean family-entertainment. "What can we do?" he mused to me. "This is what sells! This is what the public wants—sex and violence!"

We are undoubtedly in the midst of a sexual revolution; the playboy philosophy is rife. Hedonism has replaced love; self-gratification has become the *raison d'être* of our world. We are seeking new thrills—sexual aberrations included. Parents are pushing their children into premature sexual activities, and young people, writes Professor Lester Kinkendall, are trying out for themselves a "new sexual code." The results are terrifyingly real. A 1966 study predicted that if present trends continue, one of six Connecticut girls would be pregnant out of wedlock by the age of twenty. The rash of dormitory scandals at some of the posh Ivy League colleges whose dormitories have apparently been converted into breeding grounds is another indication of the new code. Polls of college students corroborate the increasingly promiscuous behavior of collegians. In 1929, 35 per cent of American college women polled admitted to pre-marital coitus, as did 50 per cent of the men. The 1953 surveys indicated a jump to 50 per cent for females and 67 per cent for males. Today's figures are disturbingly higher. A study of collegians at three New York-New Jersey schools indicated that only 8 per cent had never engaged in sexual relations.

The results of the new sexual morality are appalling: one of every eighteen children is born out of wedlock; almost one of three marriages ends in divorce; thirteen million children live in broken homes. And we have not come full cycle yet: Homosexuals are battling to receive legal recognition (they are now legitimate in England!), and other new aberrations are in the offing.

Americans are almost as preoccupied with violence as with sex. All one has to do is tune in practically any television program in order to see a spate of war shows, Western programs, gangster shows, etc. Sadism is the mood; the gun has become the TV trade mark. Who knows the impression such violence stamps on the minds of the young, the weak, the psychotic, the credulous? We who have witnessed the assassinations of both President John F. Kennedy and his brother Senator Robert Kennedy, as well as that of the Reverend Martin Luther King Jr., ought to think carefully about the impact of violence on the personalities of our children.

A new phenomenon that bespeaks the new morality is the dangerously proliferating drug craze. Liquor is no longer the forbidden fruit and ticket to bliss and inner peace (although we must not forget America's five million alcoholics!). Today we "turn off, tune in, and drop out" with drugs like marijuana, cocaine, and heroin. Even better: the new psychedelic drugs (notably LSD) are effective, non-addictive, and fashionable. It is difficult to gauge the extent of narcotics-use in the country today, and estimates vary. Some studies on college campuses indicate that drugs are relegating sex to second place in student interest. Over 25 per cent of a sampling of students at three metropolitan New York colleges admitted to experimentation with drugs. A Gallup Poll was more conservative in its findings; but it concluded that probably 300,000 collegians have tried drugs at least once. Even high schools and posh prep schools have been affected. An investigation of a high school in Westport, Connecticut, disclosed that 18 per cent of the 1,396 students acknowledged at least one experience with marijuana. The damage to mind and body is unbelievably severe; the damage to society and societal norms is stunning. The soaring crime rate is doubtlessly due, in part, to the proliferation of drug use and addiction.

All Americans decry the soaring crime rate; they are not so unanimous in decrying the fact that private honesty has taken a sharp downward turn in our land. Symptomatically, many believe that it is fair to cheat the government out of taxes. When labor racketeer Dave Beck was convicted for tax evasion of $240,000, he blithely argued that "it's happening all over America." It has been estimated that taxes could be reduced 40 per cent if everyone paid honestly and fairly.

Insurance companies are also fair game. False claims, fraudulently-padded bills, dishonest and inflated estimates —these are the order of the day.

Pilfering by employees and shoplifting at super-markets and in department stores (80 per cent of whose patrons are gentle females!) cost billions of dollars yearly, cut profits in half, and raise food prices 15 per cent. In its first year of operation, New York's Americana Hotel lost 38,000 demitasse spoons, 18,000 towels, 355 silver coffee pots, 1,500 silver finger bowls—and 100 Bibles! Most Americans seem to believe that "it's all right to cheat the big companies" since "they can afford to pay." But in the long run it is *we* who pay, both financially and ethically.

Dishonesty is evident on the campuses. Cheating by collegians is rife; hundreds of our finest boys have been discharged from the Service Academies for cheating on exams; and they are but a fraction of the culprits in colleges.

What is behind it all? Why does it appear that every area of American life is slipping perceptibly into the muck of corruption and perversion? What are the factors making for the new morality?

First of all, we should recognize that we are not confronting a "new" morality: we are merely battling sodomy in modern garb. We are in the midst of a new turn of the cycle. Victorianism replaced the libertinism of the Age of Enlightenment; now unbridled *laissez faire* has displaced prudish Victorianism. And I suppose—and pray—that the cycle will turn back to sanity before the losses mount too dangerously.

Perhaps the greatest and most grievous blow to American morality has come from World War II. Man was taught to kill his fellowman ruthlessly and efficiently; life and property were held cheap. Children grew up without fathers and became a "shookup generation." OPA violations were so rife that Prohibition paled by comparison. We became accustomed, I suspect, to cheating and lying, to fraud and deception. Just as the heart suffers permanent damage from an invasion of rheumatic-fever germs, so was the moral and ethical fibre of our nation grievously impaired during the war era. And the unremitting Cold War period—the Korean War, the Vietnam conflict—has perpetuated that tragedy.

Venality and greed are further factors in the moral decline of our nation. From Billie Sol Estes and Bobby Baker to the man next door, most people worship the almighty dollar at the shrine of the "bitch-goddess of success." Our society battens on the notion of self-gratification and self-indulgence. We are as though possessed of a Dibbuk: the ends are all important; the means are justified, no matter how corrupt or evil. In the words of that nineteenth-century scoundrel, Uncle Dan Drew, "It isn't how you get your money but what you do with it that counts!" "Everybody's doing it"—we are told.

Everybody cheats on taxes.

Everybody pads expense accounts.

Everybody mislabels merchandise.

Everybody cuts corners to survive.

Finally, our moral decline can be traced to the decline of religion as a factor in personal lives, and the separation of religion from ethics. We tend to identify religion only with prayer and ritual. We are content to go to synagogue or church, confess our sins and utter our liturgy, and check our moral faith at the door so that the next day we can proceed to rob and plunder and lie with equanimity. We have lost sight of the fact that religion and ethics are one and inseparable; that to be religious means to be honest and fair, just and merciful, pure and upright. "Who will stand on the mountain of the Lord and who will rise to His holy place? He who has clean hands and a pure heart. He who has not taken My name in vain and has not sworn deceitfully." [1]

There are those who argue that we must find a *new* moral code, that we cannot turn back to earlier, more rigid patterns, but must find a code that will fit the requirements of the new society. Others maintain the need for "situational" ethics—ethics that will fluctuate according to the demands of the moment and of the circumstances.

Judaism rejects emphatically both proposals. It decries the seekers of a new moral code and asks: "What is obsolete about the Ten Commandments or the Golden Rule?" This is not to say that standards of morality need no periodic adjustments. In fact, they do. Once Jews thought it lewd for a woman to appear publicly with uncovered hair. Today, very few zealots would hold to that attitude. Likewise, the Bible viewed usury as a religious crime. But latter-day scholars developed various legal fictions to allow the practice.

Yet, the basic rules are eternal and binding. Without an objective standard of morality and an eternally-binding notion of right and wrong, what future is there for civilization? What chance is there for stable and abiding moral norms?

Jewish tradition spurns the notion of a quixotic, situational ethic that will vary with the needs of the hour or the goals of a nation. The Germans, after all, believed it perfectly moral to kill Jews; the Russians think it legal to jail people for expressing unpopular views. If we follow a philosophy that "each man may do what seems right in his own eyes," then we end up with a crazy-quilt pattern of morality, a vagary of right and wrong that would destroy what little sense of conscience still flickers dimly in man's breast.

Judaism is predicated on the notion of ethical monotheism. It was founded on the belief that man must be ethical and honest *not* because it is expedient or utilitarian or profitable but because God demands it of us all, and because it is man's best hope. The Jew is expected to be moral because that is what religion is all about. The Prophets of Israel taught us that morality is the essence of Judaism, and that ritual without inner piety is blasphemy.

> *To what purpose is the multitude of your sacrifices unto Me? saith the Lord. . . . Bring no more vain oblations; it is an offering of abomination unto me; new moon and Sabbath, the holding of convocations —I cannot endure iniquity along with the solemn assembly. . . . Learn to do well; seek justice, relieve the oppressed, judge the fatherless, plead for the widow.*[2]

> *I hate, I despise your feasts, and I will take no delight in your solemn assemblies. . . . Take away from Me the noise of your songs; and let Me not hear the melody of your psalteries. But let justice well up as waters, and righteousness as a mighty stream.*[3]

> *If you but thoroughly mend your ways and your doings; if you thoroughly execute justice between a man and his neighbor; if you oppress not the stranger, the fatherless, and the widow, and shed not innocent blood in this place, neither walk after other gods to your hurt; then I will cause you to dwell in this place, in the land that I gave to your fathers for ever and ever. . . . Will you steal, murder, and commit adultery, and swear falsely . . . and come and stand before Me in this house, whereupon My name is called,*

and say: "We are delivered," that you may do all these abominations? [4]

Behold, you fast for strife and contention, and to smite with the fist of wickedness; . . . Is such the fast that I have chosen? . . . Is not this the fast that I have chosen? To loose the fetters of wickedness, to undo the bonds of the yoke, and let the oppressed go free . . . and deal your bread to the hungry and bring the poor cast out to your house and when you see the naked, that you cover him? [5]

The Prophets were not alone in their passion for honesty and truth, for social justice and moral conduct. The tripartite sources of Jewish law and lore—Torah, prophetic teachings, and Wisdom Literature—all contain ethical emphasis. In Torah literature, the Pentateuch exhorts us to lead holy lives because God is holy.[6] "Justice, justice shall you pursue." [7] "Love your neighbor as yourself." [8] "One law shall there be for you—both for citizen and foreigner as well." [9] And Wisdom Literature (from a more pragmatic vantage, to be sure) also underscores the need for morality.

Lord, who shall sojourn in Your tabernacle? Who shall dwell in your holy mountain? He who walks uprightly, and works righteousness, and speaks truth in his heart; who has no slander on his tongue, nor does evil to his fellow nor takes up a reproach against his neighbor. [10]

There are six things which the Lord hates, Yea seven which are an abomination unto Him: Haughty eyes, a lying tongue, and hands that shed innocent blood; a heart that devises wicked thoughts, feet that are swift in running to evil; a false witness that breathes lies, and he who sows discord among brethren.[11]

The Biblical authors were contemptuous of the pious hypocrite who rushed to the Temple on the Sabbath and festivals and resumed his rapaciousness and dishonesty the next day. Rabbinic Judaism followed the same pattern. Contrary to the libel disseminated by Christian detractors and "higher criticism," Pharisaic Judaism was not merely ossified, pilpulistic legalism concerned only with fine points of ritual law and tortuous, hair-splitting casuistry. Ethics occupy an enormous area of rabbinic literature, and the sages were acutely sensitive to the need for moral relations between man and man, which they considered even more vital than man's relationship to God. The first question to be asked of us all in the next life when we stand before God for judgment, said Rava, is this: "Did you deal honestly with your fellow-man?"

Torah study must be accompanied at all times by *derekh eretz*—literally, "the way of the world." This is a multifaceted concept that includes honest business dealings, chastity, good manners, charitable deeds, and loving interpersonal relations.

Perhaps the noblest expression of the quintessence of ethical religion was by Micah: [12] "It has been told to you O man, what is good and what the Lord requires of you; to do justice, love mercy, and walk humbly with your God."

Each of these three ethical ideals enumerated by Micah constitutes a pillar of Judaism—and, in fact, of all religions. Together they form an inseparable, three-fold cord.

Justice (*mishpat, tzedek*) is first in Micah's formulation. It is the foundation of all ethical relationships. We cannot all *love* our neighbors; we can, however, deal justly with them. The Prophets were justice-intoxicated men; the Pharisees were impassioned with the ideal of righteousness and equity. Abraham's charge to his descendants is binding on Jews in all ages: "They shall keep the way of the Lord to do justice and righteousness." [13]

Justice must prevail in all human relations. It must be done in the courts. Rich and poor, mighty and weak must receive equal treatment before the law.[14] Judges must be fair and impartial; bribery is utterly taboo.[15] Any judge who performs his duty honestly and equitably is considered "a partner with God in the creation of the universe." [16]

Justice must guide our dealings in the world of commerce as well. In business, the entrepreneur must be honest: He may not mislabel, shortchange, falsify weights or measures, sell shoddy merchandise, deceive his customer, or charge excessive prices.[17] Nor may he corner the market in order to raise prices in unfair, monopolistic competition.[18] The Romans preached: *Caveat emptor* (Let the buyer beware!). The Jews maintain: "Let the seller be fair!"

Justice must reign supreme in labor relations: The employer must deal fairly with his workers; he must pay them on time and treat them equitably in accordance with local practice.[19] On the other hand, the worker must follow the instructions of the employer, or else be liable for damages; [20] he may not utilize his work time for personal matters—not even for Torah study—because he thereby steals hours from the boss.[21]

Justice is a *sine qua non* for all of life, since the world stands on the three pillars of "justice, truth, and peace."

Our "yes" must be "yes" and our "no" must be "no;" a man's word must be his bond, and his pledge sacred. We are commanded to remove ourselves far away from false-hood [22] because God's seal is truth.[23] Deception of any kind, whether against Jew or gentile, individual or government, constitutes *hillul ha-Shem* (desecration of God's sacred name). We must pay taxes honestly because "the law of the kingdom is law." [24] God abhors those who say one thing verbally while inwardly intending to do otherwise.[25] A man's inner character should correspond to his outer actions.

Yet, despite Judaism's insistence on justice, the saintly person does not insist on pressing his full legal rights: he approaches, but does not push up to, the line of the law (*lifnim meshurat ha-din*); he tempers steely justice with velvety equity and mercy.

The second ethical strand in Judaism's tapestry as Micah defined it is mercy (*hesed*)—a derivative of the Golden Rule to love one's neighbor. "There are three qualities exhibited by the Jewish People: they are merciful, humble, and perform deeds of loving kindness." [26] "The world stands on three pillars" observed Simeon the Righteous: "Torah, Divine Worship, and deeds of loving kindness." [27] God is frequently depicted as a loving Deity, full of compassion and mercy: In fact, one of the more popular rabbinic epithets for God—often found in liturgical selections—is *ha-Rahaman* (the Merciful One).

Man is expected to imitate God, to emulate His ways. And the Jew is exhorted that "just as He is compassionate and merciful, so shall you be compassionate and merciful." [28] How does a man emulate God? "By clothing the naked, by visiting the sick, by comforting the mourners, and by burying the dead," is the answer of the sages. There are other ways in which man becomes God-like through loving deeds: He must give charity (*tzedakah* means "justice," "love," and "charity"); he must be hospitable; he must aid the poor and downtrodden, the orphans and widows. "Open your hand to your needy brother," declared the Bible, for he *is* your brother. In the words of the Hassidic saint, Levi Yitzhak of Berdichev: "Only by loving one's fellowman does one truly love God."

Micah's third principle of ethics is "humbleness" (the usual translation of the Hebrew *hatznea*).

Humility is a supreme moral trait. Moses was depicted as the most humble human being. Isaiah cautioned against all forms of arrogance, either individual or national. Hillel deliberately took a back seat in the academy lest he appear haughty. He often remarked: "When I exalt myself I am humbled, but when I humble myself I am exalted." A famous Hassidic saying is this: "A man should carry two verses in his pockets: One should read, 'Behold, I am dust and ashes;' the other should read, 'For me was the world created.' "

The Hebrew *hatznea* also means "purity, chastity." Micah was undoubtedly urging his listeners to a pure and chaste life, for Judaism is built on these values.

Sexual purity is deeply rooted in our tradition. Adultery is prohibited in the Ten Commandments. Incest is considered an "abomination," as are other aberrations like sodomy, homosexuality, zoophilia, pederasty, sacred prostitution, and transvestism.[29] As we have noted, the rabbis considered sexual immorality one of the three basic and most heinous sins. Impure speech is almost in the same category as obscene action. The spoken word is holy; man may not profane it by breaking an oath, by perjury, or by lewd talk.[30] "Those who use foul speech," cautioned the sages, "are headed for Hell." [31] The slanderers and gossipers are similarly condemned.[32] The sages go so far as to compare such sinners to lepers. In fact, the famous moralist Hafetz Haim wrote a special book entitled *Guarding the Tongue*, in which he lists twenty-eight commandments we break every time we malign our neighbor. Truly, the power of life and death is in the tongue; consequently, the Jew prays thrice daily: "God, guard my tongue from evil and my lips from speaking guile."

The pure life also precludes drunkenness and debauchery. Isaiah was disgusted by drunken princes who misled the people.[33] Hosea was equally revolted by their disgraceful spectacles.[34] Jewish tradition did not expect its adherents to be total abstainers; but it urged drinking in moderation. The sad example of Noah—debased and ruined by overindulgence in alcohol—was not lost on centuries of Jews noted for remarkable sobriety.

This, then, is not an impossible, other-worldly ethical system: It is, however, an attempt to elevate man to a point where human relations are guided by the norms of love, of justice, of truth, of humility, of purity, and of peace. "The commandments were designed to purify mankind," noted the sages. In the words of Abraham Ibn Ezra: "The essence of the commandments is to make the human heart upright." Jews are expected to be cognizant of God's presence in their midst at all times and in all situations. Immoral actions pollute both man and God, and in the long run, immoral man fouls his world as well.

Chief Justice Earl Warren delivered a stirring address at

the Jewish Theological Seminary of America in 1962 on the relationship between law and ethics. The Chief Justice stated: "In civilized life, law floats in a sea of ethics: Each is indispensable to civilization. Without law, we should be at the mercy of the least scrupulous; without ethics, law could not exist. . . ."

If we are to preserve law and order at home and abroad we must restore the ethical way of life to a position of primacy. Moral principles must be transmuted into moral action; sentiments must be actualized in deed. We need no *new* morality: We require the implementation of the *old*.

We need to attack the moral blight of our generation on every level—in the schools, in the synagogues and churches, in the labor unions and the merchants' associations.

We need conferences similar to the various White House Conferences on Aging, on Youth, etc.—conferences that would convene the leaders of government, labor, business, religion, and education to develop new interpretations of old moral codes that would cover new exigencies and develop new norms.

The curriculum of every school in the land should include readings in ethical literature. The Jewish School should engage in ethical culture—mining the nuggets of moralists such as Bahia ibn Pakuda, Moses Haim Luzzatto, and Israel Salanter. Ethical literature should be translated into English for use in adult education courses and home reading.

Above all, the home must reaffirm its commitment to the moral way of life, for it is in the home that a nation finds its strength; it is in the home that children—those tiny mirrors reflecting parental patterns—learn to distinguish between right and wrong, to love their neighbor, and to be loyal to their homes and heritage.

On all levels, then, we ought battle to create an image of moral excellence. The struggle is not easy: it is, in fact, a grim one, but moral warfare can be won if we do not lose sight of the weapons God has given us. In John Greenleaf Whittier's words:

> *. . . In God's own might*
> *We gird us for the coming fight.*
> *And, strong in Him whose cause is ours*
> *In conflict with unholy powers,*
> *We grasp the weapons He has given—*
> *The Light and Truth and Love of Heaven.*

Time ticks irrevocably on for our society. As Dr. Louis Finkelstein puts it: "The problem is not so much whether civilization will survive as whether there will be a civilization worth saving." Before we destroy ourselves inwardly; before we end up like Sodom and Gomorrah—those two iniquitous cities whose end was fire and ashes—or the decadent, rotted Roman Empire, we ought to take a long, hard look at our civilization and make it worth saving for the generations to come.

Edmund Burke once remarked that all that is necessary for the forces of evil to triumph in this world is for enough good men to sit back and do nothing. This is hardly the time for inertia and indifference. This is, rather, the moment when all good people are summoned to take up the challenge to re-kindle the spark of decency that lies within our breasts. The risks are great; the rewards are even greater.

NOTES

1 Psalms 24:3f.
2 Isaiah 1:11, 13, 17
3 Amos 5:21, 23, 24
4 Jeremiah 7:5-10
5 Isaiah 58:4-7
6 Leviticus 19:2
7 Deuteronomy 16:20
8 Leviticus 19:18
9 Exodus 12:49; Numbers 15:16, 29
10 Psalms 15:1-3
11 Proverbs 6:16-19
12 Micah 6:8
13 Genesis 18:19
14 Exodus 23:3,6
15 Exodus 23:8
16 Mekilta II, 179
17 Leviticus 19:35f; Deuteronomy 25:14ff; Baba Metziah 49a, 61b; M. Baba Batra V,10
18 Baba Batra 90b
19 Leviticus 19:13; Deuteronomy 24:14 ff; Baba Metziah 111a; M. Baba Metziah VII, 1
20 Baba Metziah 78a, b
21 Exodus Rabbah XIII, 1; Taanit 23a,b
22 Exodus 23:7
23 Yoma 69b
24 Baba Kama 113a, *passim*
25 Pesahim 113b
26 Yevamot 79b
27 Avot I,2
28 Sifré on Deuteronomy 11:22, § 49, p. 85a; Shabbat 133b, *passim*
29 Leviticus 18, 20; Deuteronomy 28:18 ff.
30 Exodus 20:7; Leviticus 19:11f., *passim*
31 Shabbat 33a on Isaiah 9:17
32 Leviticus 19:16
33 Isaiah 28: 1-8
34 Hosea 4:11, 18; 7:4

XII

War and Peace

"Peace, peace—but there is no peace!"
JEREMIAH 6:14

A parable from ancient India:

Once there were four brothers, each of whom mastered a specialty.

"I have mastered a science," said the first, "which makes it possible for me, even if I have nothing but a piece of bone of some creature, to create straightaway the flesh that goes with it."

"I," said the second, "know how to grow that creature's skin and hair, if there is flesh on its bones."

The third said, "I am able to create its limbs, if I have the flesh, the skin, and the hair."

"And I," concluded the fourth, "know how to give life to that creature, if its form is complete with limbs."

Thereupon the four brothers went into the jungle to find a piece of bone so that they could demonstrate their specialties. As fate would have it, the bone they found was a lion's, but they did not know it.

One added flesh, the second added hide and hair, the third made limbs, and the fourth gave the lion life.

Shaking its heavy mane, the beast arose, opened its ferocious mouth with a roar, and in an instant attacked its creators. He killed them all and vanished contentedly into the jungle.

Is this not the parable of man? With ingenuity and genius, with zeal and inventiveness, man has used his brawn and brain, his specialties and techniques to create instruments of murder, instruments that ultimately destroy him.

Cain and Abel started the process at the dawn of man, and each generation has improved and refined on the art.

Why? Why must man maim and kill and war? Why must he utilize his genius for destruction?

Sigmund Freud believed that aggression is a natural drive in man—an expression of the innate death wish.

Konrad Lorenz notes in his extraordinary volume *On Aggression*, that the only creatures that have failed to inhibit their intra-specific aggressions are the rat—and man.

And Judaism interprets man's penchant for aggression as an expression of the *yetzer ha-ra*—the innate, almost endemic drive to evil in all of our breasts.

Whatever the cause, one thing is certain: War is a pathetic part of man, a crucial flaw in his nature, a lacuna in his evolution.

According to one student of the question of war and peace, since 3,600 B.C.E. there have been 14,531 wars. In all the recorded centuries of history, there have been only 292 years of peace. Since World War II, mankind has been afflicted with approximately 50 wars of various proportions. The statistical average is 2.94 new wars per year from 1945 to the present; the past average was 2.61.

And at what a fearsome price! How much property has been destroyed? How many have died? How many fine

young men have been cut down in the flower of their
youth? How many innocent women and children have
suffered? How much potential and untapped genius has
been snuffed out by a bullet or arrow, a whiff of gas, a
searing flame? In our own time how many millions have
been marched off like cattle to the slaughter before a
strangely silent, indifferent world? "The barbarism of our
time," writes Herbert J. Muller, "is the more appalling because so many people are not really appalled by it." *Ecce
homo!*

If man believed Armageddon near in the past, *a fortiori*
must he believe it today, in the age of the Bomb. As the late
President John F. Kennedy put it: "Every man, woman,
and child lives under a nuclear sword of Damocles, hanging
by the slenderest of threads, capable of being cut at any
moment by accident, miscalculation, or madness." And the
father of the Atomic Bomb, the late Professor J. Robert
Oppenheimer, described our situation as that of "two scor-
pions in a bottle" for "none of us can count on having
enough living to bury our dead" in the event of a nuclear
holocaust.

How lethal is the Bomb? How calamitous would a nuclear war be?

Tragically, we have some test cases as evidence: They
are the obliterated cities of Hiroshima and Nagasaki, incinerated in August, 1945.

The weapons dropped on those ill-fated communities
were puny by present-day standards. Each bomb was only
two kilotons—twenty thousand tons of TNT—and yet,
about eighty thousand died in each city, and hundreds of
thousands were injured. The lethal radius of radiation at
Hiroshima was three quarters of a mile. People hundreds of

miles away were blinded. A third of the deaths were due to the force and heat of the blast. The firestorm (which burns and asphyxiates) created winds of thirty to forty miles an hour and burned out a five-square-mile area in twelve hours and smoldered for three days. Subsequent studies have shown an enormous increase in leukemia among the *hibakusha* (survivors) of the Hiroshima blast, not to mention genetic deformities, physical ailments, and perpetual weakness.

All of this is insignificant when compared to today's nuclear weaponry. Man has made enormous strides since 1945. We live in what Ralph E. Lapp calls the "Age of Overkill." In 1960 we had ten tons of atomic dynamite for every man, woman, and child on earth. Dr. Lapp estimates we have enough megatons (million tons of explosives) to destroy the Russians twenty-five times over. A single plane can deliver a bomb with explosive power as large as the total amount of high-power explosives dropped on Germany and Japan in *all* of World War II.

The Russians now have 100 megaton bombs in their arsenal. What would such a weapon do if it were dropped, say, on New York City?

This million-ton blockbuster would create total destruction within twelve miles of ground zero. Half the total population would die *at once* from heat and blast. Wooden structures would topple as far as 30 miles away from the detonation area. The firestorm would sear an area of 11,300 square miles (larger than Vermont), and radioactive fallout would blanket 30,000 square miles.

Fallout is one of the most frightening and long-lived effects of a nuclear explosion. For many years scientists have realized the lethal effect of radioactive materials. Some of the early pioneers in nuclear physics paid with their lives; they died agonizing deaths from the invisible but lethal rays emanating from nuclear materials such as radium, uranium, and plutonium.

Radiologists have warned us of this danger. Geneticists have cautioned us about the hazard to unborn fetuses and embryos, as well as to reproductive organs. Dr. Herman J. Muller, Nobel Laureate in genetics writes: "It is no longer a matter of doubt among scientists working in this field that radiation of the type derived from radioactive substances of x-ray machines does produce permanent changes, mutations, in the hereditary constitution of living things of all kinds."

There are varied types of lethal rays emitted by nuclear explosions. Gamma rays and neutrons cause radiation sickness and death. Strontium 90 enters the bone marrow through cow's milk and causes leukemia, even years later. Cesium 137 destroys soft tissue. Carbon 14 misshapes the genes. Iodine 131 enters the thyroid and causes thyroid cancer.

Every nuclear test spreads a fallout of these poisons over thousands of miles, in water, grass, vegetables, fruits, fish, and ultimately, in man himself.

The Eniwetok Hydrogen Bomb tests of 1954 contaminated 7,000 square miles. A Japanese fishing boat, the "Lucky Dragon," was 90 miles east of the shots. The crewmen were doused by fallout and fell ill with radiation sickness. The catch of tuna fish was polluted. The fish were discarded. But the men . . . ?

Is there a "safe" threshhold for radiation?

Professor Robert Rugh, radiologist at Columbia University's medical school says, not really: as little as ten roentgens are fatal to an embryo *in utero*. At Eniwetok, the Bomb left a thousand roentgens per hour, and twelve hours later two hundred roentgens were still radiating.

Professor Linus Pauling, Nobel Laureate in Chemistry, calculates that the tests of 1962 will ultimately result in 286,000 deformed children and over 2,000,000 deformed fetuses.

The United Nations Scientific Committee on the Effects of Atomic Radiation concluded *unanimously* (November 20, 1962) that fallout is lethal. Undoubtedly this report impelled both our country and Russia to conclude the pact barring nuclear testing in the atmosphere.

While we have banned atmospheric testing, underground testing proceeds apace. We are building better and more sophisticated bombs and missiles. We can now destroy almost entire nations. We are told that a 1,500 megaton attack would kill 60,000,000 Americans; that a 50,000 megaton attack would end life in the United States or Russia. The first Hydrogen Bomb (November 1, 1952) obliterated the islet of Elugelab and left a sea-filled cavity 175 feet deep and a mile in diameter. Imagine what the new weapon could do to London or Moscow or New York!

That there is a very real danger of a nuclear holocaust is apparent to all but the most naïve or misinformed. Such a conflict could occur, writes Professor Amitai Etzioni, in several ways. It could happen by accident or false alarm. A misinterpreted blip on a radar screen, a nuclear bomb dropped by accident, a failure of the "fail-safe" mechanism in a SAC bomber, a human or mechanical mistake. . . .

We have ample and frightening proof of such possibilities. In 1952 a false alarm set off by a flight of American B-47's nearly sent our SAC bombers winging with their lethal cargo to Russia. Several years later, A B-52 accidentally dropped a 24-megaton bomb over North Carolina, and five of six interlocking safety devices were set off. In 1960, a false radar alarm that indicated missiles headed for our country was set off by the moon.

In January, 1966, a bomber crashed at Palomares, Spain, and dropped three hydrogen bombs on land and one at sea. The accident touched off an intense and bizarre international search for the missing weapons. Thank God the weapons did not detonate! Crops were contaminated, however, and the plutonium that seeped out at sea formed a lethal hydroxide precipitate that was surely ingested by fish, and will ultimately be consumed by man.

In January, 1967, a drone missile accidentally flew over Cuba from Florida. Happily, no damage or shooting resulted.

There have been at least fifty known nuclear or missile accidents caused by American weaponry. We can only speculate as to the Russian mishaps. But with only fifteen minutes required for a missile to travel from Russia to America, the margin of error is too slim for comfort.

A second possibility of nuclear war could come from unwarranted action. A mentally deranged SAC officer, an overwrought, over-zealous missile commander could plunge us all into hell. As the tensions of the Cold War become more and more unbearable, as the nerves of nations and leaders and soldiers become more and more frayed, such possibilities must perforce multiply. Dr. Erich Fromm wonders about the psychological damage of living constantly under the threat of holocaust. The greater that damage, the longer the tension, the greater the possibility that someone just might push that lethal button.

War could also be precipitated by the strategy of brinkmanship. This peculiar term—popularized by the late John Foster Dulles—is a variation on the idea of gambling. You walk to the brink with your opponent, you go as far as you can to the abyss, you push as far as you are able, you challenge as vigorously as you dare. And you hope and pray that your opponent will give in before you both take that plunge.

We were all witness to this frightening game of "nuclear chicken" in the Cuban missile crisis. Happily, Mr. Khrushchev chickened out, and the world was granted a reprieve.

There is another way in which Armageddon can come: It can come because of nuclear proliferation. America, Russia, and England no longer have a nuclear monopoly. France and Red China have entered the nuclear club; other nations—perhaps as many as a dozen—can do so on short order and relatively cheaply. The more weapons there are, the more buttons there are to be pushed. The more buttons there are, the more possibilities there are of unwarranted, insane, accidental, insidious calamity.

Finally, a nuclear conflict could come about by escalation. Let us take the Vietnam struggle as a case in point. If America fails to win, or at least gain, a satisfactory truce, she may be sorely tempted to cease the conventional approach and escalate to nuclear weapons. Some advisors have urged this. In Korea we were at the brink of doing so, and the armistice came as a result. As long as limited wars are raging, however, the side that feels frustrated or in danger of losing will always be tempted to escalate from dynamite to plutonium. And if one side suspects the other is about to use nuclear weapons, it might feel impelled to make a preemptive strike and launch a preventive war.

Obviously, the danger of a nuclear confrontation is real —horribly real—and mankind sees the fulfillment of the awesome Biblical prophecy before its very eyes: "And your life shall hang in doubt before you." [1]

How do we proceed from here? What strategy must we follow?

There are those who argue that we must disarm unilaterally. If Russia refuses to submit to arms control, then let America disarm on its own and compel Russia to follow suit. This is, however, a fatuous and suicidal strategy.

At the other extreme are those who urge a preventive war, a preemptive, first strike at the Russians (and Chinese, and all other opponents in the Cold War) that would end our differences forever and impose peace by brute force.

Curiously, and almost unbelievably, Bertrand Russell urged America (October, 1946) to *compel* disarmament by nuclear blackmail in the days when we still had a monopoly on nuclear power. Professor Harold Urey agreed with Russell's view (1947).

Today such a policy is impossible militarily and indefensible morally. A first strike would surely result in what General Douglas MacArthur described as "double suicide."

The third approach is that of "multideterrence" or "strategic striking force." The high priest of this cult is Herman Kahn, Pentagon pundit, former Rand Corporation braintruster, and currently head of the Hudson Institute.

In two remarkable books, *On Thermonuclear War*, and *Thinking About the Unthinkable*, Kahn has expounded his strategy—a strategy that is more or less America's strategy today.

Kahn argues that a nuclear war is not only possible, but probable unless arms controls are instituted. He urges us to prepare realistically to fight and win such a conflict. We must develop varied weapons such as hard missiles, bombers, and polaris-toting submarines. We must scatter and diversify our arsenals to protect enough of them from attack so that we will be able to launch a crushing second strike and deter any aggressor.

Kahn is a strong advocate of anti-ballistic missiles and civil defense shelters. Unprepared, he writes, we might lose eighty million people; prepared we might suffer only forty million deaths. We can wage and win a nuclear war, he avers. We can lose twenty million killed, and rebuild in ten years; or eighty million dead, and rebuild in fifty years. Professor Edward Teller, father of the Hydrogen Bomb, believes that given tools and food we could rebuild in five years. And Professor Eugene P. Wigner who edited the Project Harbor Report (July, 1965) asserts that 80 per cent of Americans could survive (*i.e.*, forty million would die) and we could rebuild, provided we have adequate warning and proper shelters and anti-ballistic missiles.

To read Kahn and his colleagues is to enter a strange and eery world of fantasy and farrago. These nuclear experts play war games, they project scenarios, they compute megadeaths and analyze thousands of war possibilities, employing a new and macabre vocabulary. Their thesis is simple: We can fight and win a nuclear war if we prepare adequately.

This approach is not universally accepted, by any means. There are many scientists and military men who believe that there can be no winner in a nuclear clash, that the survivors will envy the dead: "Better those who died by the sword, than those who perished of famine." [2]

General Earle G. Wheeler, former Chairman of the

Joint Chiefs of Staff, is one of the men who believe that there can be no winner in a nuclear war. So is physicist Ralph E. Lapp who derides reckless nuclear strategists. "Much of the planet will become a hostile environment," avows Lapp.

The Project Harbor Report has not been accepted uncritically. Many believe it misleading and erroneous. Dr. H. Bentley Glass of Johns Hopkins, advisor to the Atomic Energy Commission, declares that only insects and bacteria would survive. Professor Harrison Brown opines that recovery from a nuclear war is impossible because the tools for recovery are too complicated, and the necessary, uncontaminated raw materials too dispersed.

The value of shelters is also a moot point. Some describe them as "expensive crematoria." Others view them as another spur to the armaments race. Still others aver that a fifty-megaton bomb planted at sea two hundred miles offshore would create a hundred-foot-high tidal wave that would drown the coastline inhabitants in their neat shelters.

There is also the moral question: May one defend the shelter with guns against intruders and refugees? The Rev. L. C. McHugh, S.J., writing in the Roman Catholic Magazine *America*, opined that one may repel by violence any would-be intruders. Many took the cue; they armed their shelters with guns. One is reminded of that horrendous scene painted by Michelangelo in the Sistine Chapel that depicts the Last Judgement, in which the damned club the weaker denizens of the inundated world as they futilely strive to escape the flood waters that will eventually engulf them anyway.

The anti-missile defense system is also a matter of debate. The cost would be enormous—perhaps as high as forty billion dollars. Former Defense Secretary Robert McNamara and many others concede that the system cannot stop all incoming missiles, and that it would spur the Russians to step up countermeasures.

If we are to actually survive a holocaust, our only chance is to burrow underground. Houses, schools, synagogues, churches, farms, factories—all must be built below earth. Thus man's progress and evolution will have come full cycle—from cave to cave, from slimepit to slimepit, from dust to dust: back to the Mousterian Era—not to see the sun again, or smell the sweet air, or touch a daisy, or spy a dragonfly in summer. . . . "And men shall go into the caves of the rocks and into the holes of the earth, from before the terror of the Lord." [3]

We have analyzed only the prospects of *nuclear* war. Equally disquieting, though far less publicized, is the possibility of *chemical* or *biological* warfare, which could be every bit as lethal to man and almost indefensible.

Nuclear weapons are, however, the best-publicized concern of man in this Age of Anxiety. And it is evident that the experts disagree whether we can fight and win such a battle, or whether we will end up like the tragically doomed creatures in Neville Shute's novel and movie, *On The Beach.*

A sobering thought was offered by the late Professor Norbert Wiener, father of cybernetics. "There is no 'expert' on thermo-nuclear war," wrote Wiener. On second thought, perhaps there are: there are the quick and the dead, the dying and the doomed of Hiroshima and Nagasaki.

It appears that the only hope for man to avoid Armageddon is arms control and eventual disarmament under a world government of law and order. Whether the United Nations can accomplish this as it is presently constituted is questionable. A world police force with adequate controls and inspection techniques, with sanctions and punitive processes, with the force of law and moral order seems the best recourse for man.

In the interim, the world needs a *détente*, a cooling off, a disengagement. This is difficult for a variety of reasons.

Fundamentally, there is a lack of trust. We mistrust the Communists because of their numerous breaches of treaties, their duplicity, and their frank avowals of world conquest through subversion and wars of liberation. They distrust us because of our intervention in Russian and Chinese affairs —an intervention that began with the Russian Revolution and extended into the era of the Cold War. We, too, have not been without sin. This discouraging lack of trust prevents us from reducing armaments and ending the nuclear race to doomsday. Trust is essential, for there is no completely and totally reliable system of arms inspection. Scientists Dr. J. Robert Oppenheimer, Leo Szilard, Soviet academician Nikolai Semenov, Secretary of State Dean Rusk, disarmament expert William C. Foster, the Pugwash International Conferences of Scientists—all agree that no fool-proof, perfect verification system exists in arms control. Cheating could exist no matter how tight the controls. And as Professor Eugene Rabinowitch notes, bombs can be destroyed, but not the knowledge of how to make them.

Still, even Herman Kahn agrees that "if we are to reach the year 2,000 or even 1975 without a cataclysm of some sort . . . we will almost undoubtedly require extensive arms control measures. . . ." In the choice between sure calamity and possible cheating, the prudent policy dictates the need to gamble for peace.

Should we discover that vital sense of international trust, however, disarmament will be frustrated by another obstacle. Former President Dwight D. Eisenhower warned America in his farewell address against the dangers of the "military-industrial complex." Tragically, almost every nation on this planet has become a warfare state whose economy is geared to military preparedness.

In 1964, the world expended 130 billion dollars for weapons, or 40 dollars per man, woman, and child on earth. In 1968, the United States spent over 70 billion dollars; the Russians over 50 billion dollars for weapons. And to this one must add enormous ancillary expenditures for defense. This is more than we allot for health, social welfare or education.

One-fifth of America's gross product is for military purposes. The first Atomic Bomb cost us 2 billion dollars to develop. Today, each 100-megaton bomb costs 1.2 million dollars; each Atlas missile (of which we have over 1,000) runs 40 million dollars; each Polaris sub with its deadly cargo of 16 Polaris missiles (we deploy over 40 of these ships) costs 110 million dollars, plus 160 million dollars for the missiles.

The Defense Department owns property upwards of 160 billion dollars. It employs 3.5 million persons including 947,000 civilians. "Tens of thousands of scientists and technicians . . . are convinced that weaponry is a way of life for themselves," writes Harrison Brown.

The Disease, Biological, and Chemical Warfare project so furtively carried on at Fort Detrick, Maryland, fills

1,300 acres, contains 75 million dollars worth of buildings, employs 120 Ph.D's, 34 D.V.M's, and 14 M.D.'s. Its budget in 1964 was about 158 million dollars. We don't even know its present budget.

Universities are engaged in war projects—projects that occupy the time and borrow the brains of thousands of scholars, scientists, graduate students, and technicians.

Above all, however, our huge industrial complex has become a great war machine. Our armaments industries are gargantuan. Moreover, they employ numerous retired military men. In 1961, for example, General Dynamics (builder of the Atlas Missiles) employed 187 retired officers, including 27 generals and admirals. The pressure lobbies they muster are awesome forces.

Congressmen and governors resist reduction in arms partly because of these pressure lobbies, but they also resist reductions because of economic crises and unemployment. Let us remember that 22 of our 50 states depend abnormally on military spending.

Evidently, we are harnessed to a war machine. America, Russia, France, China, Israel, Egypt, as well as many of the other great and small nations of the world, are trapped in a dilemma of their own creation. They want to disarm and dismantle their weapons, and they cannot. They are victims of their own military-industrial complexes. They cannot imagine a peacetime economy.

So man heads ever so steadily, ever so inexorably to doom. It is as if we were in a Greek tragedy; we seem fated, doomed, driven by forces beyond our control to blow ourselves up and pollute our planet. In Ralph E. Lapp's moving words: "The strangest aspect of our perilous time is the ominous quiet. Probably never in history has the human race looked so much like sheep marching silently to slaughter."

There is an extraordinary Italian documentary film called "Mondo Cane" which was shown in America some years ago. There is one scene I find unforgettable; it is stamped indelibly on my mind. The scene consists of film clips of the South Pacific atoll that had been obliterated by Hydrogen Bomb tests. We see thousands of gulls and terns and sandpipers. They are trying desperately to hatch their eggs. All is in vain. Only a few bring forth chicks; the rest are sterile—sacrifices on the nuclear altar.

Then there is a clip of a great sea turtle. The pathetic creature is struggling to find its way back to its habitat, the sea. But it cannot; the Bomb has disoriented it so thoroughly that it heads inland to the desert—and its death.

I see these scenes, and I see man on the day of Armageddon. And I wonder: Where, indeed, are we heading? What is to be done? What can man do to avert his doom?

If there is to be hope for man, we must, I believe, turn to Judaism and its conclusions on the matter of war and peace.

Judaism was intimately familiar with the problem. The tiny Land of Israel occupied a strategic place at the crossroads of civilizations. Frequently, the Jewish State was compressed willy-nilly between the great civilizations of the ancient world. Assyria and Egypt, Persia and Babylonia —all of the Middle-Eastern colossi tracked across that sliver of land, leaving in their wake death and destruction, pillage and pestilence. The Bible reflects those turbulent times.

At first glance the Bible seems to be a bloody chronicle, no better or more moral than the chronicles of other ancient peoples. The Pentateuch and Book of Joshua record

the brutal battles against the various nations that blocked
the way for the Hebrews to enter the Promised Land. The
Canaanites were ruthlessly expelled or wiped out; in fact,
the Hebrews believed they were divinely commanded to
annihilate the indigenous populations as well as the insidious Amalekites—the ancient enemy who had molested the
weak and the young as they trekked out of Egypt. The
Book of Deuteronomy [4] sanctions a holy war against any
Jewish community that went astray after idols.

The Book of Judges and the chronicles of the kings
record sanguinary episodes in Jewish history. Saul and
David were mighty warriors; their hands were bloodied by
numerous enemies. The later kings were, with few exceptions, little better; they were not even averse to slaying
their own kinsmen in internecine civil war.

Naturally, our forefathers engaged in defensive wars
throughout the Biblical and Graeco-Roman eras. Midianites
and Canaanites, Philistines and Egyptians, Babylonians and
Assyrians, Greeks and Romans—all tested the mettle of the
Jewish nation. That Jews fought for their freedom with
heroism and sacrifice cannot be gainsaid. Josephus' graphic
description of the life-and-death struggle against the Romans, and Professor Yigal Yadin's dramatic excavations at
Massada demonstrated the heroism in battle mustered by
our ancestors against impossible odds.

This is not the whole story, however, for even in our
early history we see a revulsion against war. The Bible reflects man's perpetual ambivalence—aggression versus
peace, death against love. The more Jews encountered battle, the more it repelled them; the more they tasted blood
and ashes, the more their great teachers, seers, and sages
sought to circumscribe the scope of war.

Thus it came about that we accepted war as a sometimes legitimate means of settling disputes, but we did so with heavy heart and guilty conscience. Consequently, as our tradition evolved, Jews became *pacific*, albeit not necessarily *pacifistic*.

Even the Pentateuch had attempted to humanize warfare and bridle man's aggressive drive.

When you go forth to battle against your enemies . . . the officers shall speak unto the people, saying: "Which man has built a new house and has not dedicated it? Let him go and return to his house, lest he die in battle and another man dedicate it. And what man is there who has planted a vineyard and has not used its fruits? Let him go and return unto his house lest he die in battle and another man use the fruits. And what man is there who has betrothed a wife and has not taken her? Let him go and return to his house lest he die in battle and another man take her." [5]

There was an incipient idea of conscientious objection, as witness this passage: "And the officers shall speak further unto the people and say: 'Which man is there who is fearful and fainthearted? Let him go and return unto his house, lest his brethren's heart melt as his heart.' " [6]

War was to be the last resort; peaceful settlements of disputes were preferred, even in the heroic age of Biblical Judaism. "When you draw near unto a city to fight against it, then proclaim peace unto it." [7]

Nor did the Deuteronomist view war as an unlimited contest ruled by the notion that "all's fair in love and war."

When you besiege a city a long time, in warring against it you shall not destroy its trees by wielding an axe against them. You may eat of them but shall not cut them down; for is the tree of the field a man that you may besiege it? Only the non-fruit trees may you cut down and destroy to make bulwark against the city. . . .[8]

The Bible's abhorrence of bloodshed is evident in the fact that notwithstanding David's fame and preeminence, he was not permitted to build the Temple at Jerusalem. Why not? Because his hands were imbrued with the blood of his many victims and he was a man of war.[9]

The yearning for peace was never more evident than in the writings of Israel's Prophets. Those great giants of the spirit, appalled by the warring empires, the brutality, the inhumanity, and the bloodshed, came to the conclusion that war is hell and peace the highest ideal.

Hosea, who lived around 740 B.C.E., was one of those prophets of peace. Professor Yehezkel Kaufmann describes him as the "first Biblical author, indeed the first man in history to condemn militarism as a religious-moral sin."

For Israel has forgotten his Maker and built palaces, and Judah has multiplied fortified cities; but I will send a fire upon his cities, and it shall devour the castles thereof.[10]

And again in chapter 10, verses 13 and 14:

You have plowed wickedness, you have reaped iniquity, you have eaten the fruit of lies; for you have

trusted in your chariotry, in the multitude of
your mighty men. Therefore shall a tumult arise
among your hosts, and all your fortresses shall be
spoiled. . . .

What more glorious repudiation of militarism as a national policy than that of Isaiah! What more exalted vision
of world peace than that of the great Seer of Jerusalem
who wrote over seven hundred years before the Christian
era!

. . . *And they shall beat their swords into plow-*
shares, and their spears into pruning-hooks; nation
shall not lift up sword against nation, neither shall
they learn war anymore.[11]

Peace plays a central role in Isaiah's messianic visions for
the future for he prophesied an end to the aggressive drive
in man and beast:

And the wolf shall dwell with the lamb, and the
leopard shall lie down with the kid . . . and the lion
shall eat straw like the ox. And the suckling shall play
on the hole of the asp, and the weaned child shall put
his hand in the basilisk's den. They shall not hurt or
destroy in all My holy mountain; for the earth shall
be full of the knowledge of the Lord, as the waters
cover the sea.[12]

Isaiah's younger contemporary, Micah, expresses similar
sentiments against a foreign policy based on war machines:
". . . I will cut off your horses out of your midst and I

will destroy your chariots. I will cut off the cities of your land and I will throw down all your strongholds." [13] And one of the last of Israel's seers, Zechariah, remonstrated with his People that victory would come "not by might nor by power but by My spirit, saith the Lord of hosts." [14]

Echoes of the prophetic denigration of militarism are found scattered throughout the Psalms as well. The Psalmists exhort their readers not to place their trust in horses and chariotry, or in armies or military might, for victory comes through matters of the spirit—and trust in the Lord.[15]

Revulsion against militarism heightened perceptibly after the Hasmonean Wars and the several revolts against Rome. It was not that the rabbis were pacifists; not that they opposed battles to the death for the sake of Torah and religious freedom. They were repelled by the bloody wars of aggression and the fratricidal contests of the Hasmonean princes. They realized the folly and futility of challenging mighty Rome for political hegemony when religious liberty was all they really sought, and all that mattered in the long run.

The sages crystallized their views in their laws and sermons, their homilies and theology. And they did so in a remarkable and bold fashion: they reinterpreted Biblical laws, lore, and history. They completely revised the biographies of Biblical heroes. And they set out to sublimate man's aggressive drives and canalize his martial instincts into constructive endeavors.

The rabbinic ideal was that of peace—peace for Israel, peace for the world. One of God's many names is said to be *shalom* (peace). The Jew greets his fellowman and bids farewell to his fellowman with the same word, *shalom*. His spiritual capital is Jerusalem, "City of Peace." Rabbi Simeon ben Yohai viewed peace as the quintessence of all blessings, the summation of all ideals and dreams. The essential achievement of the Messiah will be world peace. "Great is peace! For when the Messianic King comes he will begin his reign with peace, as it is written: 'How beautiful upon the mountains are the feet of the messenger of good tidings who announces peace. . . .' " [16]

Consequently Jews are expected to wage peace, to work for a society, as Rabbi Simeon ben Gamaliel phrased it, based on "law, truth, and peace." [17] The three are really one; for when justice is done, truth prevails, and peace is established.

How does one wage peace?

One does so on several levels and in varied ways. First of all, the pursuit of peace must be an active passion, not merely a passive dream. "Seek peace and pursue it," sang the Psalmist.[18] "This means," wrote the rabbis of the Midrash, "seek it in your community and pursue it abroad." [19] Every Jew is expected to work for peace on all levels, from the most mundane and domestic to the highest councils of nations. When one brings peace between neighbors or between a man and wife, one is sure of enjoying the rewards in the world to come.[20] Rabban Yohanan ben Zaccai, leader of the peace party in the days of the Great Revolt against Rome, is the author of this splendid homily on Exodus 20:22:

You shall build the altar of whole stones. (Deut. 27:6.) They are to be stones that establish peace. Now, by a fortiori *logic you reason: The stones for the altar do not see or hear or speak. Yet, because they*

> *serve to establish peace between Israel and their
> Father in Heaven, the Holy One, blessed be He, said:
> You shall lift up no iron tool upon them.*[21] *How
> much the more then should he who establishes peace
> between man and fellowman, between husband and
> wife, between city and city, between nation and na-
> tion, between family and family, between government
> and government, be protected so that no harm should
> come to him.*[22]

Likewise, the Jewish civilization has eschewed glorifica-
tion of war, of weaponry, of martial spirit. Jews have
never extolled the Prussian military ideal; nor have they
considered it an *honor* to die for chauvinism, for colonial-
ism, for aggression. It was not even an *honor* to die in the
defense of one's land. A brutal and bitter *task*, yes; an
honor, no.

Psychologically, we have always sought to condition our
people to shun the martial spirit and to laud the man of
peace. It is interesting to note that the sages shuddered at
the harsh ring of the "God of war" mentioned in the Bible.
They much preferred a God of peace, of justice, of love
and compassion. "At the Red Sea," they note, "God appeared as a hero doing battle, as it is said, 'The Lord is a
man of war.' [23] But at Sinai He appeared like an old man
full of compassion, as it is said, 'And they saw the God of
Israel. . . .' " [24] Often when the word "warrior" is mentioned in the Bible, the rabbis took it to mean "warriors of
Torah" whose battles were fought in the Yeshivot, and
who drew ink rather than blood. Our heroes were not soldiers on battlefields but warriors who clashed in the academies of Torah.

This explains why the sages of the Talmud totally reassessed and revised the rôles of our greatest military heroes. Thus David, Joab, Amasa, and Abner, Israel's mightiest warriors, emerge in rabbinic literature as warriors in the realm of Torah! The mercenary Cerethites and Pelethites who served David in his numerous wars are taken to stand for the Sanhedrin who advised David and legislated for the people.[25]

We had contempt for the bloody hunter and military man. Tubal-Cain was alleged to have been the fashioner of the first swords and knives.[26] Because he improved on the method of murder of his ancestor Cain, mankind's first killer, he is scorned by Jewish tradition and branded a bloody brute. So is Nimrod the hunter;[27] so, too, Ishmael, the "wild-ass-of-a-man," and Esau, the bloody hunter who "lived by the sword." "Those who live by the sword," declare the rabbinic teachers, "die by the sword."[28] The perversity of the monarchy was exemplified, according to the anti-monarchists, by the perpetual warfare the kings brought upon the people.[29]

Jews detected no beauty in the sword or spear or implement of death. On the contrary, we shunned such tools of terror:

Why was no iron implement permitted in the construction of the Sanctuary or Temple? Because iron was created to shorten man's life, whereas the altar was created to prolong man's life.[30]

Weapons are not considered decorative in Jewish tradition. Nor are they proper instruments for a Jew to use; rather are they the tools of Ishmael and Esau, of Christendom and Islam.

We can gain insights into the Jewish abhorrence of weapons of death in these legal discussions: "One may not enter a synagogue or schoolhouse with a sword in hand." The reason is, according to Rabbi David Halevy, that prayer is designed to lengthen man's days, while the sword is designed to shorten them; hence, the two are incompatible.[31] And elsewhere we are taught:

> *A man may not go out into the public domain on the Sabbath with a sword or bow or spear. Rabbi Eliezer permits it because these are his jewelry. But the sages rule that they are a disgrace to him, as it is written,*[32] *"and they shall beat their swords into plowshares. . . ."* [33]

Further evidence that Jewish tradition strove to condition its adherents to peace rather than war can be inferred from the law of the priestly chaplain. The Bible provides that a special priest be designated to exhort the armies before entering battle.[34] Rabbi Abraham Kook, late Chief Rabbi of the Holy Land, offers an acute observation. He draws our attention to the fact that the priesthood is an hereditary post; not so the chaplain-priest. Why not? Because, writes Rabbi Kook, peace is the only natural (hence, permanent) state of man. But war is at best a necessary evil and a temporary, unnatural state of affairs. Hence, the chaplain's post was *not* hereditary.

The Jewish People has for millennia clung to the notion that it has a mission to the peoples of the world. Other nations have also maintained this notion. Some have seen it as a fiat to war on barbarians; others interpreted their manifest destiny as a license to conquer in the name of God, country, Communism, or civilization. Jews never viewed their vocation in these martial terms. Legend has it that God offered Israel the choice of the Book or the Sword. If we chose the Sword, then we would destroy ourselves; if the Book, then we were assured survival and blessing. We were never to be deflected from that mission of bringing the light of morality and holiness, of justice and peace to the world. Israel's mission is to be a "Kingdom of Priests and a Holy nation" [35]—not a "warring empire builder." [36] Other peoples resort to warfare; Israel's "occupation" is the occupation of Abraham, Isaac, and Jacob—namely, prayer.[37] The Talmud records that an Angel of God rebuked Joshua for neglecting Torah study and worship in order to war on Jericho.[38]

The Jewish people, therefore, is expected to teach the world that the real heroes are the peacemakers; that disputes must be settled peacefully, that power can only be justified when tempered by justice and morality. The former Prime Minister of Israel, David ben Gurion, notes that Psalm 89:14-15 links strength inextricably with justice: "Yours is a mighty arm; strong is Your hand and exalted is Your right hand. Righteousness and justice are the foundation of Your throne; mercy and truth go before You." Without ethical reins, unbridled power degenerates into tyranny.

There are concrete strategies each Jew is expected to adopt in order to bring peace to the world and fulfill his mission. Fundamentally, the causes of aggression and war must be eliminated. We must stamp out greed, lust, injustice, bloodshed, immorality, dishonesty, religious and political fanaticism, and poverty.

Poverty is obviously a major cause of aggression and

war. The Jew has always been expected to wipe out poverty through *tzedakah* (charity). In every age, Jews have been tithed and taxed for the poor; they have maintained soup kitchens and hospices; they have shared their festival meals with the orphan and widow, the wayfarer and beggar. But Jewish law is sensitive to the fact that alms alone cannot stamp out poverty. Maimonides rules in his *Code* that the highest form of charity is to prevent poverty by loaning a person money or teaching him a trade or setting him up in business so that he becomes self-sufficient.

Moreover, conditions that make for war can be eliminated by sublimating man's aggressive drives. As we have seen, the Jew found sublimation in such things as Torah competition, scholastic battles, and scholarly rivalry. Modern man might do so in cultural competition, athletic contests, space exploration, and scientific projects.

Tensions can also be reduced by eliminating the arms race and calling a halt to the proliferation of death machines. "We may not sell iron to brigands, pirates, arms dealers, robbers, murderers, or enemy nations lest they make it into implements of war." [39] Defensive weapons (such as shields) may, opine the sages, be sold to friendly nations.

Jewish tradition insists on truthful dealings in international relations and on the sacredness of the treaty or covenant. Abraham and Isaac each had disputes with the Philistines over the ownership of wells. Each resorted to compromise rather than mayhem in order to settle the arguments. And each drew up a binding treaty of peace and mutual trust.[40] So, too, Joshua respected the treaty concluded with the Gibeonites even though it was obtained by a ruse.[41] When later generations violated the covenant, the violators were severely punished.[42] Josephus records that the High Priest at Jerusalem refused to breach his oath of allegiance to the Persian monarchy, despite the threats of the conqueror, Alexander the Great.[43] The word is sacred, and an oath must be upheld if mutual trust is to prevail.

Sometimes, however, truth must be twisted for the sake of peace. This may seem startling in view of Judaism's passion for truth. But Judaism's passion for peace is even greater. Consequently, white lies are allowed if peace is at stake. There are a number of illustrations of this concept in rabbinic tradition and there are apparently Biblical precedents for it. For example, when Sarah was informed by the three angels that she would bear a child, she laughed, and asked, "After having become old shall I have pleasure? And my master has also become old!" [44] When reporting the incident to Abraham, the Lord deletes the reference to Abraham's impotence [45] lest Abraham be angered by the insult and turn against his wife.[46]

Similarly, Joseph's brothers tampered with truth when they inform him that before his death, old father Jacob had exhorted Joseph not to harm the brothers or seek vengeance.[47] The Bible records no such last testament of Jacob; the Rabbis accordingly infer that the brothers were tampering with the facts—for the sake of peace.[48]

Jewish tradition acknowledges that *coexistence* is preferable to *no existence*. The world is filled with diverse races and religions, with varied ideologies, and with opposing doctrines. It is, consequently, essential for men to be tolerant of differences, to get to know one another in order to learn to respect those differences, and to inject a sense of humor into dangerously-charged and tense human relations. Konrad Lorenz observes that animals rarely attack members of the pack whose scent is familiar. And he notes that men rarely kill other men while laughing—unless, of course, the killers are psychopaths.

Our tradition endorses the importance of "getting to know" one another in order to understand one another. And it appreciated the role of humor in curbing aggression. Legend has it that Elijah singled out two clowns whom he spotted in the market place as worthy of the world-to-come. Why? Because whenever they saw two men arguing, or husband or wife squabbling, they soothed them with *jokes* until the cause of the conflict was forgotten.[49] One of the finest expositions of the ideal of coexistence is this passage from the Midrash:

> *Two archangels dwell together in heaven, Michael and Gabriel. One is entirely of snow; the other is entirely fire. And yet they coexist. How so? God's presence casts a state of peace on them, as it is written,*[50] *"He makes peace on high."* [51]

Only when God's presence dwells among men can "fire and snow" dwell side by side.

Another way in which Jewish law and tradition sought to curb man's aggressive drive and foster peaceful coexistence is in its stress on the amicable settlement of differences. We believe it is "better to be of the persecuted than of the persecutors;" we prefer to accept insults without retaliating in kind. And we have constantly stressed that it is preferable to save lives rather than face; that one ought *not* to insist on his full legal rights or press demands to the limit or letter of the law; that a person should forego his own dignity and prerogatives for the sake of peace.

Indeed, compromise has been the favorite technique of the rabbis or *Beth Din* (religious court) for the settlement of disputes from antiquity until today. The power of compromise was adjudged greater than that of strict justice.[52] Only when there is compromise can society strike the proper balance between justice and peace. The nations of the world might do well to ponder this ruling:

> *Two boats were about to enter a narrow canal. If both pass, they will sink; if one proceeds at a time, all will be well. Similarly, if two camels ascend a narrow mountain pass large enough for one, if both pass together they will fall; if one passes at a time, all will be well. What do we do? We permit the loaded one to go first, or the nearer one allows the further one to go first. If both are equidistant, we compromise and compensate the one who gives way.*[53]

What better way to achieve world peace than for a great power that can afford to be generous to agree to compromise or consent to waive its full legal rights! A person, a nation can be fully entitled to its demands and legal position, and yet endanger the peace. Once the porters of Rabbah bar Bar Hanah dropped some casks of wine. He seized their cloaks as payment. Rav ruled that he must return them and pay their wages. "But, why? I am entitled to the cloaks! Is this the law?" "True," answered Rav. "But you can afford to go beyond the letter of the law and not press your full rights with these poor workers." [54]

Every diplomatic means of easing friction and settling disputes amicably must be pursued. "Who is a hero? He who makes his enemy into a friend." [55] This is not an easy task: but it is far easier than bloodshed and genocide. In this regard, Aaron the High Priest serves as a paradigm for us. He was the exemplar of a peacemaker. Whenever he saw neighbors feuding or husband and wife spatting, he acted as conciliator. His technique was artless, yet effective: He pulled one party aside, smoothed down his hurt feelings, and soothingly assured him that the other party really wanted to settle the dispute. Then he took the other party aside and repeated the process. Finally, he brought the disputants together for reconciliation.[56]

War must always be the *last* resort, the *final* option when all others fail. "Better were the peaceful policies pursued by Elisha than all the wars of King Joram son of Ahab," observed one sage.[57] The Book of Deuteronomy had already enjoined the Jew to seek peace through diplomatic means at all costs. When that fails, when war becomes inevitable and peace becomes untenable, then and only then may the nation resort to war. "When you draw near unto a city to fight against it, first proclaim peace unto it." The sages stress the point that peace is preferable to war and that all efforts must be exerted to avoid bloodshed.[58] Nachmanides (Rabbi Moses ben Nachman of Spain, died in 1270) opined that Jews were to seek peace *even* with the Canaanite nations despite the Divine injunction to annihilate them.

There is a striking passage in the Midrash that suggests that Moses convinced God, so to speak, that peaceful diplomacy is preferable to war:

Rabbi Levi observed that God concurred in whatever Moses decreed. . . . The Holy One, blessed be He, ordained that Israel should war on Sihon, as it is

said ". . . and contend with him in battle." But
Moses did not do so. Rather, we are informed that
Moses ". . . sent messengers . . . unto Sihon . . .
with words of peace. . . ." The Holy One, blessed be
He, said to Moses: "Have I not commanded you to
wage war with him? And yet you opened negotiations
with peace offers. Upon your life, I will confirm your
decree! In every war, Israel will be required to first
seek peace through diplomacy." [59]

Does all of this evidence indicate that war is *never* justified? Not at all. When all else fails, the Jews realized that a
person or nation must take up arms. A civilization that believed in the injunction "Thou shalt not murder" was naturally reluctant to do so. A people conditioned to the ideal
that "one who takes a single life destroys, as it were, an entire world" would of course be most diffident about doing
battle. Yet, we were *not* pacifists; we were willing to fight
when we found no alternative. The same Abraham who
preferred compromise to war with the Philistines nevertheless went to war against the King of Sodom.

Jewish law recognizes two kinds of war: defensive war
(*milhemet mitzvah*) and offensive war (*milhemet reshut*).
Under the category of defensive wars, we have included
the battles against the seven Canaanite nations and the
Amalekites, as well as wars against invaders of the Holy
Land. In addition, we were permitted to take up arms when
attacked—even on the Sabbath—because self-defense is a
legitimate procedure and the saving of a life takes prece-
dence over the sanctity of our holiest days.[60] Permission to
wage defensive wars on the Sabbath was first granted by
the sages in Maccabean times when Judea's enemies slaugh-

tered thousands of pietists who refused to take up arms on the Lord's day.[61] Moreover, no conscientious objection is condoned in such wars for survival. "Everybody must go to battle," note the rabbis, "even a groom from his bridal chamber and a bride from under the nuptial canopy." [62] King David was allegedly the first to issue this order.[63] If a person still objects to battle and bloodshed, he may serve in an auxiliary troop, supplying water and food to the warriors and repairing roads.[64]

The question of offensive wars is more complex. In theory, such wars were sanctioned in order to spread Israel's borders and increase its prestige. Such wars, however, could only be authorized by the Great Sanhedrin of seventy-one judges in Jerusalem.[65] The Bible also permits offensive wars on Jewish communities that have been seduced into idolatry.[66] And Maimonides, doubtlessly influenced by the spirit of the Crusades and *Jihads* of his day, envisioned a Messianic King who would wage war on the idolators and enemies of God "provided that his deeds are for the sake of Heaven, that his purpose is to elevate the True Faith, and that he seeks to fill the world with justice and break the power of tyranny in waging the wars of the Lord." [67]

Nevertheless, normative Judaism sought to abolish even legitimate offensive wars. The wars against idolatrous Jewish communities were, *de jure*, still possible; *de facto*, the sages abolished them by erecting all manner of legal impediments. The notion of conscientious objection was expanded *ad absurdum* in order to curb the warlike drive. Rabbi Akivah, for example, would excuse any tenderhearted soul who feared the sight of blood, while another schoolman rules that if one soldier fears he may have committed even *one* minor sin, all return from the wars! We felt uneasy over spilling blood, even in the line of duty. At the Red Sea, legend informs us, the angels sought to sing a hallelujah. God silenced them: "My creatures [the Egyptians] are drowning and you want to sing before me?" [68]

Another legend records that Abraham's conscience troubled him after the War of the Kings.[69] He grieved over the bloodshed and feared he might have shed innocent blood. God assured him that he had shed only the blood of the wicked, that he was "weeding the garden" of the Lord.[70] And despite the justifiable vengeance of Simon and Levi in destroying the Schechemites for having defiled their sister Dinah, neither the Bible nor the Midrash excuses their bloody lynch law.[71]

It is noteworthy that Don Isaac Abravanel, financial advisor to Spanish and Portuguese monarchs and exile from Spain in 1492, writes in his Biblical commentaries that no king ought to launch a war of aggression because of moral and pragmatic considerations.

War is sometimes unavoidable, but it need not be fought with consummate brutality. Jewish law sought to mitigate war's harshness, to humanize the very inhuman act itself. As we have already noted, before besieging a town, Jewish warriors were to offer peace to the defenders. They were to leave one side of the city open so that civilians might flee the horrors of siege.[72] In addition, the soldiers were specifically enjoined not to cut down fruit trees lest the population starve to death.[73] Jewish warriors were to be kind to the survivors of battle and spare their lives (Biblical law notwithstanding) if they accepted the Seven Laws of Noah and repented their crimes and corruption.[74] Later generations felt a sense of malaise over the brutality of Biblical wars, even justifiable ones. Thus Rabbi Joshua ben Hananiah asserts that Joshua slew only the Amalekite generals and officers, taking care not to defile the corpses or utilize brutal means of execution. Rabbi Eliezar ben Hyrcanus extenuates the brutality of those wars by commenting that the Hebrews "were merely following God's decree." [75] The medieval scholar, Rabbi Abraham ben Maimonides, wrote that the brutal wars Israel waged against King Mesha of Syria resulted in the calamities showered on Israel enumerated in II Kings 3:27.

In the light of the Jewish attempts at alleviating suffering and humanizing war, it is inconceivable how any Jew can advocate blunderbuss bombings or nuclear holocaust. A war that decimates foliage, that destroys crops, that murders innocent civilians, that shatters homes and farms, that pollutes air and water—such a war is brutal beyond words. And such is the nature of thermonuclear war. But this world is *not* man's to destroy; we are merely tenants, custodians. "The earth is the Lord's and the fullness thereof." [76] Man cannot capriciously obliterate that which is not his.

How successful was Judaism in inculcating in its people the ideals of peace? Was their passion for peace merely a reflection of their impotence in military affairs after the destruction of their state?

On the whole, Jewish history is less bloody than that of its neighbors. True, Jews did engage in wars defending their lands of adoption. This was the case among German and Bohemian Jewry. It was especially true of Spanish Jewry. In fact, in 1342, Alfonso XI petitioned Pope Clement VI asking permission for Seville Jewry to use the synagogue of Don Yucaf de Ecija "for they contribute to the welfare of the city and at times even join the Christians in fighting the Moslems, and do not fear to risk their lives." Occasionally Jews even joined in aggressive battles. The eminent poet and scholar Samuel ibn Nagrela (Shmuel ha-Naggid) who died in 1056, led the Moslem armies of Granada against their enemies. But if Jews failed to adhere to the ideal of peace, it was a failure of Jews, not Judaism.

A combination of external and internal factors dissuaded Jews from military adventures. The external factor was the Diaspora itself: the feeling of alienation in often hostile lands, the sense of impotence at having no true homeland to defend, of often being denied the right to bear arms. The internal factor was the long-standing tradition of peace and abhorrence of bloodshed that conditioned Jews over the centuries to avoid war and shun violence.

Nowhere is this more clearly seen than in the Jewish Messianic ideal of the future—an ideal that reflects this psyche of the People. Israel, remarks a rabbi in the Midrash, will not be like the other nations; it will not impose its rule over them by force, but will triumph over all nations by spiritual power.[77] Maimonides notes that in the Messianic era, Judaism will not force other peoples to accept its tenets; but all men will, of their own free will, choose to walk in the ways of Torah. Jewish Messianism contains no notion of religious imperialism, of conversion to Judaism by force.

So much for the Jewish concept of war and peace. How can it be of value to modern man? It can be of inestimable value to modern man because of the needs of the hour.

What is needed in meeting today's unprecedented and

radical threat to human survival is an unprecedented and radical change in man and society. This is the very essence of the Jewish Messianic ideal.

Man needs a new heart—a heart in which God's law of love, justice, morality, and peace will be implanted forever. It is of such a "new" man that Jeremiah, Isaiah, and Ezekiel spoke and dreamed. "The tragedy of war is that it uses man's best to do man's worst," wrote Harry E. Fosdick. Israel's prophets and seers, sages and scholars envisioned a new man whose talents and genius would be harnessed to building, not destroying, to loving, not killing. Man needs a new heart and spirit if he is to preserve the hard won gains of civilization. He needs to curb and channelize his aggressive drives and develop what William James called the "moral equivalents of war."

We must also create a new society—a society based on freedom, not slavery; on justice, not oppression; on internationalism, rather than unbridled chauvinism; on interdependence; not egoistic independence. Governments must be established on a new system of righteousness, for "righteousness exalts a nation." [78] National policy must be constructed on superstructures of mercy and truth, as the Psalmist says: "When mercy and truth meet, then righteousness and peace kiss." [79]

International affairs must be governed by international cooperation; unbridled nationalism must yield to supranationalism. The Prophets envisioned a Messianic future when ancient enemies would be united in trust and friendship.

In that day shall there be a highway out of Egypt to Assyria, and the Assyrian shall come into Egypt, and the Egyptian into Assyria; and the Egyptians shall

*worship with the Assyrians. In that day shall Israel be
the third with Egypt and with Assyria, a blessing in
the midst of the earth. And the Lord of hosts will
bless him saying: "Blessed be Egypt My people and
Assyria the work of My hands, and Israel mine inheritance."* [80]

Isaiah prophesied an end to national rivalries, to petty
jealousies, to nationalistic feuds that tear man assunder.
Some day, he believed, all flesh would come on Sabbath
and New Moons to worship the Lord.[81] And Zephaniah
went further: his Messianic vision was for a return to man's
pristine state prior to the Tower of Babel, when all men
were of one people and one speech. In the new era, sang
the Prophet, God will cause all the peoples to speak "a pure
language, that they may all call upon the name of the Lord
and serve Him shoulder to shoulder." [82] This dream of
truly united nations, of one family of man, finds noble expression in the liturgy of the Jewish prayer book. There we
find the ideal of "one band of men serving God with perfect heart." What more splendid summation of the Jewish
goal of coexistence and one world than the third-century
alenu prayer recited daily by devout Jews:

*We hope for the day when the world will be perfected under the kingdom of the Almighty, and all
mankind call upon Your name. . . . May all the inhabitants of the world perceive and know that unto
You every knee must bend, every tongue vow loyalty. . . .*

Finally, world peace must be preserved through world
law and international morality. War must no longer be an

instrument of foreign policy. The affairs of nations must not be governed by the law of the jungle, by international nihilism and anarchy, by a philosophy that each man, each nation does what is right in its own eyes for the sake of selfish interests. This notion of world law is also part of the Jewish Messianic dream of a new heaven and a new earth, a new man and a new society.

> *And many peoples shall go and say: "Come, let us go to the mountain of the Lord, to the house of the God of Jacob; and He will teach us of His ways, and we will walk in His paths." For out of Zion shall go forth the Torah, and the word of the Lord from Jerusalem.*[83]

Time is running out. Every year we inch ever closer to the precipice, to calamity, to doom. We must create a new man and a new world if there is to be a man left in this world. Other creatures of God have disappeared, other civilizations have become extinct. Will man join their ranks? Will our civilization prevail?

The answers, I believe, depend on our acceptance of the Jewish ideal of peace.

NOTES

[1] Deuteronomy 28:66
[2] Lamentations 4:9
[3] Isaiah 2:19
[4] Deuteronomy 13:14 ff.
[5] Deuteronomy 20:1-7
[6] Deuteronomy 20:8
[7] Deuteronomy 20:10

[8] Deuteronomy 20:19f.
[9] I Chronicles 22:8, 28:2 ff.
[10] Hosea 8:14
[11] Isaiah 2:4; cf. Micah 4:1-4
[12] Isaiah 11:6-9
[13] Micah 5:9f.
[14] Micah 4:6

15 Psalms 20, 33, 147 etc.
16 Isaiah 52:7; Leviticus Rabbah IX, 9, end
17 Avot I, 18
18 Psalms 34:13
19 Leviticus Rabbah IX, 9
20 M. Peah I,1
21 Deuteronomy 27:5
22 Mekilta II, 290
23 Exodus 15:3
24 Mekilta II, 21
25 Berakhot 4a
26 Genesis 4:22; Genesis Rabbah XXIII, 3
27 Genesis 10:8f; Genesis Rabbah XXXVII, 2-3
28 Tanhuma *Lekh Lekha* § 7, p. 32b on Psalm 37:14-15
29 I Samuel 8:20; Sanhedrin 20b; Rashi *ad loc.*
30 Exodus 22:22; Mekilta II, 290; M. Middot III, 4; Avot V, 8, etc.
31 Sanhedrin 82a; *Orah Hayim* 151, 6; *Taz ad loc.*
32 Isaiah 2:4
33 Shabbat 63a; Yer. Shabbat VI, 4; 8b
34 Deuteronomy 20:2-4
35 Exodus 19:6
36 Mekilta II, 205
37 Mekilta I, 205ff. on Exodus 14:10
38 Megillah 3a on Joshua 5:15f.
39 Tosefta Avodah Zarah II, 1; Avodah Zarah 15b, 16a; Yer. Avodah Zarah I, 6,7; 39c
40 Genesis 21:23; 26:29
41 Joshua 9:15, 19
42 II Samuel 21
43 *Antiquities* XI, 8,3
44 Genesis 18:12
45 Genesis 18:13
46 Leviticus Rabbah IX, 9; Baba Metziah 23b
47 Genesis 50:16f.
48 Genesis Rabbah *ad locum;* Berakhot 27b; Sanhedrin 107b; Yevamot 65b; and other illustrations

49 Taanit 22a
50 Job 25:2
51 Sifré Deuteronomy § 199, p. 111a; Deuteronomy Rabbah V, 12, and *passim*
52 Sanhedrin 5b, 6b
53 Sanhedrin 32b
54 Baba Metzia 83a; Rashi *ad locum*
55 Avot de Rabbi Nathan XXIII, p. 75
56 Avot I, 12; Avot de Rabbi Nathan XII, pp. 48 and 51; Sanhedrin 6b on Malachi 2:6
57 Seder Eliahu Rabbah p. 39 on Koheleth 9:18 and II Kings 6:20-23
58 Deuteronomy 20:10; Sifré Deut. § 199, p. 111a
59 Deuteronomy Rabbah V, 13, end on Deuteronomy 2:24
60 Mekilta III, 197f; Yoma 84; Sanhedrin 72, etc.
61 I Maccabees 2:29-41; II Maccabes 5:25 ff.
62 Sifré Deuteronomy § 198, p. 111a; M. Sotah VIII, end; Sotah 44b; Yer. Sotah VIII, 10; 23a, etc.
63 Louis Ginzberg, *Legends of the Jews,* VI, 51
64 Sifré Deuteronomy § 193, pp. 110a,b
65 Sotah VIII, 42-44; Yer. Sotah VIII, 10, 23a; Sanhedrin 20b, etc.
66 Deuteronomy 12:14f.
67 Maimonides, *Code,* "Kings" IV, 10; cf. XI, 4, and the possible source in Sifré Numbers § 84, p. 22b
68 Tosefta Sotah VII, 14; Sanhedrin 39b; Megillah 10b
69 Genesis 14
70 Genesis Rabbah XXXXIV, 4; Tanhuma *Lekh Lekha* § 19, I, pp. 38a, 38b
71 Genesis 34:30;49:5f; Genesis Rabbah LXXX, 2, and *passim*

72 Sifré Numbers § 157, p. 59b; Maimonides, *Code*, "Kings," VI, 7

73 Deuteronomy 20:19; Sifré Deuteronomy § 203, p. 111b; Baba Kama 91bf; Maimonides, *Code*, *op. cit.*, VI, 8-11

74 Sifré Deuteronomy § 202, p. 111a; Sotah 35b

75 Mekilta II, 146f.

76 Psalms 24:1

77 Midrash Tehillim on Psalm 122, p. 253a

78 Proverbs 14:34

79 Psalms 85:11

80 Isaiah 19:23-25

81 Isaiah 66:23

82 Isaiah 3:9; cf. Genesis 11:1-9

83 Isaiah 2:3

Afterword

I HAVE tried in the preceding pages to discuss some of the great issues that confront man in this Atomic Age. And I have endeavored to examine them in the light of Jewish tradition—seeking, when possible, a Jewish approach to the problems that plague all men and all nations on this planet. In doing so, I have set forth the classical Jewish sources so that they may speak for themselves.

I have attempted (perhaps not always successfully) to avoid the three cardinal errors that frequently ensnare spokesmen of religions and interpreters of religious traditions. Those errors are: arrogance, irrelevance, and unintelligibility.

Arrogance is perhaps the fallacy of most religious traditions. It is a philosophy that teaches its adherents to proclaim, "We are wise, and the Law of the Lord is our possession." [1] Such smug self-righteousness and pietistic prating distort mankind's vision and pervert its concept of truth. Consequently, we must come to the realization that each of the great faiths of man has some insight, some sparks of genius, some beacon light to illumine our night of despair, and that none are infallible or omniscient. I do not believe that Judaism has the keys to the Kingdom, or that it holds forth the answers to all of humanity's problems; nor do I concede to my Christian or Moslem or Buddhist neighbor the right to laud his monopoly on truth over the rest of us "infidels."

Religion must adopt a little more humility (a virtue it commends to others but eschews in itself) and a good deal more magnanimity if it is to be restored to its former significance in human affairs and if we are to improve interreligious relations. Mankind needs less external piety, less other-worldly salvation, fewer platitudes about saving man's soul, and more dynamism and imagination in saving his body and his world. I am frankly fearful of the man who proclaims: "Brother, I have come to save your soul." Beware that man! He is apt to take your life in the process of saving your soul. I commend to the reader the advice of the Kotzker Rebbe: "A man should worry about his own soul—and his neighbor's body."

Irrelevancy is, unquestionably, the second failing of religion. Religion has been for too long the tail of the dog. It has, unfortunately, too often told the people what they *wanted* to hear, speaking "smooth words" and avoiding "controversial issues." [2] Religion has joined the people rather than demanding that the people join *it* with heart and soul. But now modern man cries out not for sacerdotal officials, not for ritual directors, not for esoteric, archaic, chanting priests. He yearns, instead, for a dynamic, prophetic faith—a faith that speaks to all in the idiom of our time, that deals forthrightly with the issues of day-to-day life, and that is prepared courageously and intrepidly to rock the boats of our ease and contentment, our complacency and egoism. If the message of religion is to pierce the shell of man's intransigence, it must be relevant, meaningful, and pertinent.

The final problem is one of communication, of intelligibility, of knowledge. Religion can only be effective in changing human behavior and societal patterns if it is known, intelligible, and understood. That is why I believe that Judaism's message ought to be heard. It is, after all, the mother of two universal faiths that number over a billion adherents. If (as Judah Halevy argues so cogently in his *Kuzari*) Islam and Christianity have distorted the original message and failed to effect man's salvation, perhaps it is time to turn to the original. Surely Judaism can do no worse than its inept daughters. Who knows? It might, given half a chance, improve on the dismal record of the past. It is, conceivably, man's last and best hope. . . .

If, however, Judaism is to fill this saving role, then it has to be known, studied, and publicized by and for Jews—and gentiles. Its relevancy and modernity have to be disseminated. It may *not* remain a fossil, a museum piece, a curious antique to be admired at a distance but never touched or handled.

And that is what this book has been all about.

NOTES

1 Jeremiah 8:8   2 Cf. Isaiah 30:15